MY LOVE AFFAIR WITH

MOVIES

Other books by Anita Weinreb Katz

Psychoanalysis In Fashion
by Anita Weinreb Katz and Arlene Kramer Richards
published by IPBooks Inc © 2017

Advanced Praise for

MY LOVE AFFAIR WITH M O V I E S

❧❧❧

In *My Love Affair with Movies*, Dr. Anita Katz invites us to explore two of her passions—movies and a deeper understanding of human relationships. In this book, Dr. Katz takes us through a series of films from various parts of the world that she has found deeply moving through the years, describing them with strong emotion and then bringing them to life again....as portrayals of human beings in all their depth and complexity.

~ Herbert H. Stein, MD—Faculty Member of the Psychoanalytic Association of New York (PANY); Author of over 50 essays on psychoanalysis and film published in the PANY Bulletin, many of which were republished in Moving Pictures: Films Through a Psychoanalytic Lens by Herbert H. Stein. (IPBooks 2017) and Double Feature: Discovering Our Hidden Fantasies in Film by Herbert H. Stein (EReads, 2002 and Open Road Media (Kindle Edition), 2014)

❧❧❧

My Love Affair with Movies is an excellent beacon for all who are interested in understanding what movies mean to them. Dr. Anita Katz, starting with some seminal films which particularly intrigued her, studies them through a solid psychoanalytic perspective as clinical data "in terms of dialogue, events, affect, and behavior, all in the context of the ongoing life situation and historical data available". Anita's sensitive, rich and deep commentaries can be enjoyed, not only by professionals, but by teachers and students, and, above all, by everyone who would like to enter into the psychic complexity of other worlds grasping "its multitude of feelings and thoughts—crying, laughing, celebrating, mourning, losing, finding".

~ Franco Borgogno, Training and Supervising Psychoanalyst of the Italian Psychoanalytical Society, Past Full Professor in Clinical Psychology (Turin University), 2010 Sigourney Award Recipient. His most recent book is One Life Heals Another: Beginnings, Maturity, and Outcomes of a Vocation, published by IPBooks.

MY LOVE AFFAIR WITH

M O V I E S

Understanding Films on the Surface, and Diving Deeper

Anita Weinreb Katz

IPBOOKS.net
International Psychoanalytic Books

International Psychoanalytic Books (IPBooks)
New York • IPBooks.net

MY LOVE AFFAIR WITH MOVIES
Understanding Films on the Surface and Diving Deeper
by Anita Weinreb Katz

Published by IPBooks Inc
International Psychoanalytic Books
Queens, New York
Online at www.IPBooks.net

ISBN: 978-1-949093-91-9

Editing, Cover Design, Layout & Typesetting by lisa roma
Original "Balloon Girl" Cover Artwork and frameable page by Banksy, Copyright © 2021 by Banksy. Used with permission.
All photographs copyright © 2021 Anita Weinreb Katz
Back cover photo of Anita Katz by Joel Matalon © 2021

DEDICATION

♦

This book is dedicated to my daughter, Jennifer Melissa Katz, a veterinarian, who at age nine convinced me to get a dog, promising that a dog would be no trouble for me since she would walk it. Of course, that didn't happen.

The dog, named Christopher Robin by Jennifer, joined me in my office and proved to be a wonderful co-therapist. One of my patient's greetings, in fact, was, "Hello, Dr. Katz. Hello, Dr. Dog."

Jennifer (who is now Dr. Katz, a veterinarian) has challenged and inspired me, to love, laugh, and cry, and has shown me what it means to be human. She has deeply enriched my life.

Shanta Genia & Jennifer

BALLOON GIRL by BANKSY © 2021

"Unconditional Love: Dr. Katz & Dr. Dog (Christopher Robin)"

ACKNOWLEDGEMENTS ∞

To begin with, I thank Arlene Kramer Richards who has inspired and encouraged me to embark on professional writing. We have collaborated on several books, and this is my first solo flight.

This book is in memory of my brother, Marvin Weinreb, who was a dermatologist and philanthropist. Twice a year, he flew his two-engine airplane to Baja, Mexico as a member of Flying Doctors of California to administer volunteer medical care for indigenous Mexicans. For a six-month period, he flew to North Africa with his wife, Ilene, former mayor of Hayward, CA. She taught modern methods of using computers, and he taught modern methods of medicine. His crew included other medical professionals and family members, including his daughter, Rachel, a pediatrician, and our brother, Joseph, a retired policeman, who gave eye exams with an eye chart and provided the eyeglasses to patients who needed them.

I am grateful to my mother, Minna Banges Weinreb, for giving me the gift of music, which helps me write. She was a concert pianist whose performances were aired on the classical radio station WQXR. And I am grateful to my father, Samuel Weinreb, a pharmacist who owned his own pharmacy, and was astounded and proud to learn that his daughter had some smarts. And to my younger brother, Joseph Weinreb, who was fun to be with and made me feel grown-up. We are a musical family. My older brother played violin, my younger brother played clarinet, I played piano. And my father played the radio but was an amazing audience.

I would like to thank all my teachers and friends who thought I was smart and appreciated my ability to write. Life is full of contradictions. When I was three years old, I remember my father saying, "We have one smart one," (my older brother, then six), "and one dumb one" (me). That was because I was not interested in reading; I was more interested in playing with dolls, coloring and drawing. However, that did have an effect on me for a long time. It was not until second grade, when the teacher praised my reading abilities, did I feel I was not dumb.

After my father's retirement, he traveled from New Jersey to New York University (NYU) to help me collate my dissertation data. Working side by side with my father was a wonderful and unexpected experience. (One summer as an undergrad, I worked in my father's drug store, selling cosmetics.)

One of my most thrilling experiences with my Dad was on the day we went to my doctoral graduation. At that time he expressed an awesome appreciation of his daughter, who he now believed had lots of smarts. Before returning my cap and gown, my father put them on, and I photographed him. He looked great.

I want to thank Ira Katz, the father of my daughter, Jennifer. He gave me the gift of being a mother, and the privilege of witnessing our daughter Jennifer, develop from birth thru childhood and evolve into a remarkable woman, in her personal life, and profession as a veterinarian.

Many thanks to Lisa Roma, whose astute editing and layout design are important contributions to this book. Her literary expertise and professional and personal support assisted me every step of the way and helped me expand my vision. She is great to work with.

And last, but in no way least, my many thanks to Banksy, for gracing the cover of my book, and adding a special frameable page, with his inimitable artwork.

Anita Weinreb Katz

Anita's Family Photos

Dad in his Pharmacy

Anita and Grandma

Mom & Grandma

Mom playing piano

Mom & Grandpa

*With love
at the center
of it all*

Bubbe and Zaide

Grandpa outside his Hardware

Anita and Jenny

Anita's Family Photos

Anita Dancing

**Anita with Brother Joseph &
Grand-Niece Hannah**

Jenny & Anita

Brother Joseph & Anita

Brother Marvin & wife Ilene

Joe & Annie

Anita with brothers Marvin & Joe

TABLE OF CONTENTS ⊂℞ Page

PREFACE ❧

Every Saturday during my teens, I went to the movies by myself where I was transported into another world.

While walking home, I was immersed in the movie I had just seen, often identifying with one of the characters. I continued to remain in the world of the movie for many hours, during supper, and until I went to sleep.

It is not surprising that my interest in movies foretold my chosen profession as a psychoanalyst. I observe and listen to people and try to understand them on a deeper level. Understanding people, their motivations, dilemmas, hopes, desires, and fears, are so often the subject of the movies that intrigue me. The difference is in my role as psychotherapist I will have an impact on the course of their life.

The movies I've chosen to include in this book have enlightened, impressed, moved and entertained me. Some of them are disturbing but deal with important issues of being human. I have tried to represent the totality of the human experience.

Writing this book has been a journey much like working with someone in psychotherapy. The exceptional power of movies has helped me to go deeper into understanding the human condition.

I share my journey in writing this book with all who are interested in understanding what movies mean to them.

Anita Weinreb Katz

INTRODUCTION ℛ

Movies sometimes require us to let go of our usual state of mind and invite us to enter worlds that contains a multitude of emotional, geographical and interpersonal landscapes. There are times when we have an empathic connection with the characters and their conflicts, and other times when it is harder to empathize with them. However you "splice" it, films speak to us in an all-encompassing way that is much different from reading a book. Films transport us; it is like being there.

Films enable us to think about some experiences without the consequences of going out and enacting them. For me, this is not a retreat from living my own life, but an enrichment, an education—sometimes fun, and sometimes scary, and sometimes heart-wrenching.

In this book I will delve into several movies that move me in ways that I just described.

Psychoanalytic Study of Films: The Meanings and Complexities of Being Human

Movies offer outlets for dealing with anger, murderous feelings, sexual feelings, love, joy, sorrow, pain, as well as interpersonal and intrapersonal conflict. Trying to understand the characters in a movie gratifies my curiosity about people's motivations, fears, pleasures, and conflicts. They help me to understand the human condition in all its multitude of contexts—challenges, relationships, dilemmas, and pleasures, both very different from my own, and in some ways very similar to my own.

As a teenager, I often walked home still engrossed in the movie I had just seen (and lived through). I identified with the character that most appealed to me—either for her loving behavior, her gumption in expressing her feelings and opinions, knowing how to get the man she wanted, the loving or interesting friendships she cultivated, and knowing the way to protect herself from noxious people. Some film

1

characters inspired me to have the courage and determination to overcome obstacles that would have stopped me from doing and experiencing things I longed for.

Movies continue to inspire me. A recent example is the movie "*Rocketman*" which portrays the life and musical genius of Elton John. Playing piano captivated him from a very early age, something his innate musical genius enabled him to do. My deep connection to Elton John was unquestionably related to my mother's exceptional musical talent. She was a celebrated concert pianist, and though professing not to like popular music, could and would play by ear any popular song that I sang. Sometimes I would improvise a dance to her music. It was a wonderful duo—a magical connection to my mother in contrast to the tempestuous times with her.

Elton John's parents never appreciated his exceptional musical talents. In spite of his brutal childhood, or maybe because of it, he was driven to play and create his own music. By having the courage and passion to follow his dreams, his exceptional musical talent was developed and expressed. This enabled him to accomplish amazing music in spite of a tumultuous childhood that sometimes put him in harm's way. After a period of craziness, he eventually settled down with love and tranquility in his life.

Rocketman, the movie, and the amazing person, Elton John, are an inspiration and an affirmation to me for following my unique journey in life. Writing this book is a part of that journey.

Anita Weinreb Katz

CHAPTER ONE ‎ ❦

Film Previews: Coming Attractions

Following are brief film summaries preceding my in-depth psychoanalytic film studies. The films that are included in this book are:

The Vanishing, directed by George Sluizer, (1988); *A Woman Under the Influence,* directed by John Cassavetes (1974); *Utz* directed by George Sluizer (1992); *American Beauty*, directed by Sam Mendes (1999); *Proof,* directed by Jocelyn Moorhouse (1991); *Lust, Caution* directed by Ang Lee (2007); *The Piano Teacher,* directed by Michael Haneke (2001); *Damage*, directed by Louis Malle (1992); and *Father of the Bride*, 1950, directed by Vincente Minelli, and the 1991 version directed by Charles Shyer.

My Process

When I write about a film, I watch it multiple times and return to certain segments repeatedly. In order to do so, I require my own copy of the film so that I could watch it multiple times.

In the case of the film *The Vanishing*, I contacted the distributer who was also immensely intrigued by this movie. We talked for many hours about it. One day, I got a phone call from a man saying he represented Mr. Sluizer, and he wanted to know what motivated my interest in his film. I said that I would be happy to give him that information, but that it would be better if I could speak directly to Mr. Sluizer. He said he would convey that to Mr. Sluizer.

Not too long afterward, to my delight, I received a phone call from George Sluizer himself. He asked me what interested me in his film, and I said that I would be happy to tell him, but that it would be better to discuss it in person. We set up a meeting, and it unexpectedly went on for many hours. We both grew hungry and ordered dinner, each of us intrigued by the other. He was curious about the psychoanalyst who was captivated by his film, and wanted to understand and write about it, and I was curious about the director who created the movie, *The Vanishing,* one of the most intriguing movies that I had ever seen.

In Chapter Five, I discuss the original Dutch version of the film *The Vanishing (Spoorloos)* with English subtitles, directed by George Sluizer, as a springboard for delving into psychoanalytic issues of intimacy.

The data in this chapter derive from a close study of the first fifteen minutes of this film, which depicts two lovers, Saskia and Rex, driving from Holland to France on holiday. The verbal and nonverbal portrayal of their experience and a repetitive dream of one of the lovers are included in this segment of the film.

Finally, my way of using films offers a new way of teaching psychoanalytic process and concepts. By closely monitoring the film, or film clips, all participants involved in this shared material can learn about his or her unique contributions and reactions to the material, as well as study concepts such as fetish, transitional phenomena, screen memories, traumatic loss and intra-psychic effects, and factors that facilitate change.

The Vanishing (Spoorloos) ~ directed by George Sluizer (1988)

The first movie that I was inspired to write about is *The Vanishing, (Spoorloos),* a film originally created by the Dutch director George Sluizer. This film is both terrifying and incredibly intriguing. I needed to understand the connections between love, hate, intimacy and danger that this film portrays in a vivid and compelling way.

The main characters are a Dutch couple traveling on vacation in France. The mishaps and dangers that they encounter become more and more ominous. The juxtaposition of love and danger are powerful and intriguing aspects of this film, as they are in life.

The Dream is About Claustrophobia

My understanding of Claustrophobia is seen as a characterological issue related to intimacy. Thus, the dangers associated with the experience of "too little" or "too much" space between self and other are discussed in relation to claustrophobia. On one end of the continuum, too little space between self and other is associated with fear of being swallowed up. Too much space between self and other is associated with fear of abandonment.

In this film, intimacy is portrayed in terms of gender issues and the following defenses and fears: claustrophobia, fear of abandonment, fear of being controlled—or worse, "swallowed up"—passive aggressiveness, and sadomasochism.

In my discussion of this segment of the data, these fears and defenses are linked to the trauma that occurs in the movie. These behaviors and defenses are discussed as manifestations of pathological intimacy. This kind of intimacy puts the two lovers at risk and forecloses the possibility of an authentic dialogue between them. When their alliance with each other is fractured, they become angry and fearful of being betrayed or annihilated by the other. Paradoxically, because they are then vulnerable, they become fragile and needy of each other to shore them up. They both become decompensated, and the conclusion of this movie is powerful and frighteningly tragic.

A Woman Under the Influence ~ directed by John Cassavetes (1974)

This film's main character, Mabel Longhetti, is a fragile, playful, childlike lonely woman, beautifully played by Gena Rowlands. She knows how to play with children, have fun with them and enter their fantasy life. She is a good mother and is loved by her children. Her husband, Nick, is a tough, macho working-class guy (played by Peter Falk) who does not understand his wife and her vulnerability.

In this study, I hope to convey to the reader an understanding of the main character's strengths and weaknesses, as well as her joys and pains, and how she was misunderstood, both by her husband and the psychiatrist. Because of this, she was sent to a mental hospital, not in the spirit of understanding her fears, fantasies, conflicts and desires, but rather as a label or designation of craziness. It was delightful to watch her playfulness with children, and very painful to watch her being treated as weird and crazy by her husband and a neighbor.

Utz ~ directed by George Sluizer (1992)

George Sluizer's 1992 dramatic film, *Utz,* portrays a significant period in Central European history between 1967 to 1968. The film explores the meanings and experiences of repetitive and dramatic enactments of love, conflict, and loss, as played out with the protagonist's precious collection of Meisen pottery. The protagonist, Utz, relives his own fantasies through ritualistic play with the Meisen figurines. In addition, he is obsessed with opera divas, perhaps a throwback to his earlier more privileged life as a Baron. The live-in housekeeper lovingly takes care of him and is witness to his obsessive play. Both his and her losses, as well as their love for each other are indirectly and dynamically played out through the dramatic enactments with the Meisen pottery.

American Beauty ~ directed by Sam Mendes (1999)

In this study of the movie, *American Beauty*, I will focus on the developmental journey of parents in tangent with the developmental journeys of their children. I propose that parents revisit their own adolescent passions, conflicts and separation issues when faced with similar issues in their adolescent child. This regression tests the parents' old solutions and offers the chance of discovering more mature and fulfilling resolutions of revisited desires and conflicts, as demonstrated by Jane's parents, Carolyn and Lester Burnham, in the film *American Beauty.*

But this movie portrays that the adolescent revisitation in a parent has a dark side as well. For Ricky's father, Colonel Fitz, his rigid homophobic controls collapse when his passions are reawakened by his son's physical and psychological maturation. Because Colonel Fitz cannot bear to know what is inside of himself, his brittle adjustment cracks, and he decompensates, regressing to more primitive and violent ways of dealing with reawakened passions and conflicts.

Proof ~ directed by John Madden (2005)

In this chapter, I examine the interplay between loss of one aspect of self, functioning eyesight, and the physical and emotional loss of the most important person in this boy's life, his mother, when he was 10 years old. I use my experience with the film, *Proof*, to study the relationship between physical and psychic loss, and to study the process of healing. This film presents us with the paradox of a blind photographer. He takes photos in order to "see" and know, and at the same time to keep secrets and lie to himself.

The film prods us to reexamine concepts of seeing and nowing, visa-vis inner and outer space, and to study the interplay between psychic and external reality. I examine this film in terms that parallel what is healing or curative in the analytic process.

The film is used to demonstrate how both the protagonist and his therapeutic partner grow in the process of their encounter. Similarly, once the analyst is open to the patient as a separate person, the analyst's inner world shifts as well, and he or she is also changed. I also examine this film in terms of the protagonist's use of his camera and the photos he takes.

This film also demonstrates that the same object(s), i.e. camera and photos, can be used as fetish or transitional object depending upon whom it is used with. This has implications for the analytic process in which the analyst serves as camera and mirror to help unravel the feelings and mysteries in the conscious and unconscious mind of the patient.

Lust, Caution ~ directed by Ang Lee (2007)

Lust, Caution is a movie that hones-in on the psychology of collaborators and resistors—in this instance, related to the invasion of Shanghai by Japan—but focusing on the Chinese collaborators and the Chinese resistors.

Before I saw this movie, I did not understand as much about the people themselves who become collaborators on the one hand, or those who become part of the resistance movement.

This movie beautifully and poignantly depicts the passions, fears, disappointments, vulnerabilities and inner conflicts of these people—perhaps portraying more in depth regarding those who joined an active resistance movement than those who became collaborators.

The Piano Teacher ~ directed by Michael Haneke (2001)

Michael Haneke's film *The Piano Teacher* (2001) is a viscerally clenching and disturbing, dark cinematic portrayal of enmeshment, repression, sadism, masochism and destruction counterpointed by the soaring romantic music (composed by Martin Achenbach) that infuses the dramatic narrative. Underlying and informing the tight and conflicted characterization of Erika Kohut, the piano teacher, portrayed by Isabelle Huppert, lies the dark labyrinth of mother-daughter bonds and bondage.

The Piano Teacher explores dialectical tensions between dependency and autonomy, creativity and destructiveness, longing and deadness, innocence and sexual perversion, psychosis and repressive control. Symbolic of these dialectical tensions is the fact that most of the film's scenes are either set in formal, elegant and sophisticated settings that are evocative of the cultural gatherings of Vienna, or in raunchy, sordid settings.

The Piano Teacher shows a life in which the exquisite humanism of the music that Erika plays and teaches cannot save her tormented soul. *The Piano Teacher* is a painful portrayal of how artistic genius can be perverted at the hands of a twisted mother-daughter relationship, enmeshed in a sadomasochistic "pas de deux".

Damage ~ directed by Louis Malle (1992)

The Vanishing ~ directed by George Sluizer (1988)

Father of the Bride (originally directed by Vincente Minnelli (1950); remake directed by Charles Shyer (1991)

I discuss the three films, *The Vanishing, Damage,* and *Father of the Bride,* to study and illustrate the way the same phenomenon can appear in a number of different men, and in different variations. Awareness of this possibility enhances our understanding and clinical work with men and with their daughters. The phenomenon is the Oedipus complex, in which fathers and daughters "fall in love" with each other, and the daughter is competitive with the mother. This happens, according to Freud, in the first Oedipal stage (ages 3-5) and in the second (ages 11-13).

Finally, my way of using films offers a new way of teaching psychoanalytic process and concepts. By closely monitoring the film, or film clips, all participants involved in this shared material can learn about his or her unique contributions and reactions to the material, as well as study concepts such as fetish, transitional phenomena, screen memories, traumatic loss and intra-psychic effects, and factors that facilitate change.

CHAPTER TWO ‽

A Woman Under the Influence
Directed by John Cassavetes (1974)

Faces of Abuse: Portrait of a Couple

A Psychoanalytic Study of the Film *"A Woman Under the Influence"*

The ground-breaking film, *A Woman Under the Influence*, written and directed by John Cassavetes, came out in 1974, long before domestic abuse became a prominent issue. It portrays a woman and man struggling with inner and outer demons for psychic survival, for connectedness and separateness, as well as for love, gratification, and recognition.

In a 1996 *Filmmaker* magazine poll of people in the film industry, the fifty most important American independent films were chosen. *A Woman Under the Influence* was placed in the number one slot.

My focus is on the intrapsychic and interpersonal issues, conflicts, and processes that contribute to understanding domestic violence. At the opening of the film, the lens zooms in on a vulnerable couple, Mabel and Nick. Mabel (portrayed by Gena Rowlands) is a homemaker who is very attractive, intense, and animated. She is devoted to her husband and three children. Nick (portrayed by Peter Falk) is an attractive, appealing man who works as the head of a city construction crew. He is devoted to his wife and children. The cast includes Mabel's mother and father, Nick's mother, Nick's buddies at work, and a psychiatrist. The detailed synopsis that follows is the data from which my clinical understanding is derived.

Synopsis

The film begins with the children being picked up by their maternal grandmother so that Mabel and Nick can spend an evening and the next day alone with each other. Mabel worries that her mother won't call her if one of them "is bleeding."

An emergency at Nick's work requires his team to work all night. His vigorous protests to his supervisor are dismissed. His date with Mabel cannot be kept. He avoids calling her for several hours, afraid of her reaction. When Eddy, his friend, understands Nick's reluctance as his fear of the storm of Mabel's emotions, Nick protests: "Mabel's not crazy. She cleans the bathroom, and takes care of the kids, like a normal person. I think I know what's wrong with her, she's mad at me." But the next moment, he says, "She's wacko."

The scene shifts back to Mabel, at home alone. She takes a dress out of a box, lays it on the bed, and turns on opera music, preparing for her night out with her husband. She drinks; she smokes. When Nick finally calls her, she grimaces and reassures him that it's fine.

After this conversation, Mabel goes to a bar. She picks up a good-looking stranger. She says: "Nick stood me up after my mother took the kids," wanting to be heard, soothed, and recognized. Instead, the stranger takes her home and rapes her.

Upon awakening in her bed the next morning, she addresses the stranger who raped her as "Nick!" He replies "No, Garson Cross. I am the one who brought you home last night." *She opens a door marked "PRIVATE," and goes into the bathroom.* She comes out of the bathroom, and spunkily asserts, "I'm not in the mood for games, Nick." Pointing to him—"Nick Longetti," and then pointing to herself, "Mabel Longetti." He leaves, ironically feeling rejected and used by her.

Nick then walks in flanked by twelve buddies from work. He innocently jollies her: "Whatsamatter?" Instead of answering him, she playfully pulls his hat down over his eyes. She sweetly asks if he is hungry. Neither mention the night before. *She goes into the bathroom,* and when she comes out she warmly welcomes the twelve men. Some warmly hug her; some flirt with her. She prepares spaghetti, sits down with them, and tries to make conversation. Nick, competing for attention, observes that there are periods when no babies are born, and then all of a sudden, periods when lots of babies are born. He is convinced it has to do with "something in the air." His friends are uneasy and try to humor him, but he holds on to his theory.

Mabel is intrigued when one of the men beautifully sings "Celeste Ai'da." She gets up to stand next to him. Gazing at him, she listens enraptured. Nick is fixed on her from his place at the opposite end of the table. She tells a Chinese man: "I love this face," and asks him to sing. When he says he can't sing, she asks him to dance, "everybody can dance." He refuses her invitation, but she continues relentlessly. Nick gently says: "That's enough, Mabel; you've had your fun." She ignores Nick's repeated urging to stop and to sit down. Finally Nick screams: "Get your ass down!" She sits down grimacing, silenced. At that moment, his mother calls complaining of a stomach-ache, and Nick is very concerned and caring.

The men leave. Mabel and Nick sit down at opposite ends of the table. Mabel gesticulates and makes faces and noises. Nick calls her "wacko." She mimics him—"Get your ass down! I was trying to be nice; I'm a warm person. I love those guys. I know how to make them feel comfortable." Nick says "What the hell you talkin' about! You didn't do anything wrong." She, again mimicking, spews: "Sit down Mabel!" He: "I know—but he [the Chinese man] didn't know. He thought you meant something by it. I don't mind you being a lunatic." She pleads, "I didn't do anything wrong." Nick throws her a kiss. In her confusion, she transforms, shifting from rage and hurt to sweetness, saying: "Nick, don't be afraid to hurt my feelings. Tell me what you want me to be. [magically gesturing] I can be that. I can be anything!"

We then hear opera music, and they go to bed. Nick kisses her; she averts her face; he continues affectionately. She neither objects nor actively participates. Later on, while they are still in bed, her mother barges in, returning the children six hours early because one of them had forgotten a book for school. Mabel upon seeing her mother angrily screams, "What are you doing here?" She jumps out of bed and *goes into the bathroom*. Her mother ignores her and cozies up to Nick. Nick invites the kids to jump into bed with him and play, and then drags his mother-in-law into bed as well—meanwhile ignoring Mabel's words of concern about the children needing to get to school on time.

15

Her entreaties to her mother to go promptly and to Nick to stop playing with the kids are ignored. Nick opposes Mabel's urging the kids to leave, addressing her plaintively as "Ma." She is furious. "Don't call me Ma, Nick; my name is Mabel. I don't like to be called 'Ma'." Nick enjoys playing with the kids. Mabel sits apart from them on the bed, silently grimacing and gesticulating. After a few minutes she jumps out of bed and says with enthusiasm: "I've got a great idea, kids; we're gonna have a party when you come home from school. But you've got to leave now." At this they all jump out of bed and run out of the house with grandma trailing behind.

After Mabel's triumph, she passionately jumps into bed on top of Nick. He immediately asks, "Are you alright? Are you gonna be all right?" thereby killing the love connection initiated by her. She finally says, "What do you think, I'm wacko or something?" She jumps out of bed and says, "I can't wait until my kids come home. All of a sudden I miss everybody."

In the next scene, Mabel is impatiently waiting for her kids at the bus stop. Aggressively demanding the time from several well-dressed passing women, who recoil. She responds with hostile name-calling.

We then see Mabel joyously greeting her children. "I hope you kids never grow up—never. I never did anything in my life that was anything except I made you guys." She asks them, "Tell the truth, do you ever think of me as dopey or mean?" Her son answers, "Oh no, you're smart and pretty—and nervous." She feels known and accepted and thanks him. She tells her children, "You see, we know how to talk to each other."

In the next scene, her children are visited by three friends who are dropped off by their father, Mr. Jenkins. Mabel insists on the father staying to join the fun, i.e., dancing, playing. Aware of his discomfort, she hopes to make him comfortable. When her efforts fail, she gets nasty with him, ridiculing his stiffness and his name. He abruptly leaves with his kids, but not before a physical confrontation with Nick, who has just come home with his mother and finds Mr. Jenkins in the upstairs bedroom where all the kids and Mabel are gathered. He screams, "What are you doing in my room? Get out!" Mabel tries to intervene; he slaps her and blames Mr. Jenkins, "You see what you made me do? Get out!" Mr. Jenkins yells: "I'm tired of you, your wife,

16

and your whole family!" Nick lunges for him, and he knocks Nick on the couch. Nick's mother jumps on top of him to keep him from fighting, afraid he will "kill" Mr. Jenkins. His mother is appalled at the chaos.

In the next scene, Nick and his mother are anxiously awaiting the arrival of the psychiatrist. They have planned Mabel's commitment to a psychiatric hospital. They all agree that Mabel is crazy. She suspects their conspiracy to imprison her. She tries to reason with Nick, to reassure him that he loves her, that he didn't even hurt her when he hit her, and she loves him. "I said it [the marriage] is gonna work because I'm already pregnant." Nick tries to shut her up. Mabel won't let him shut her up. "They can't pull us apart…. We're supposed to be on the inside and them on the outside," desperately pleading with him not to abandon her.

At that moment, the doctor enters, blows her a kiss and says, "Gee, Mabel, you're beautiful." She poignantly pleads her case: "Nobody here needs a doctor" and humorously interjects, "I had the hiccups a while ago, but they're gone now…. I know I sometimes drink; I do have anxieties, but I'm a good mother, a good person—not bad nor crazy." The psychiatrist tells her there's nothing to worry about, asking Mabel if he could have a drink. Magically, Mabel's face lights up delighted, suddenly believing the unbelievable—that he is making a social call, and that he's her ally.

Nick's mother cruelly lashes out at her, screeching, "You give him nothing—you're empty inside!" Mabel screams back at her. Nick's mother screams at the doctor to calm Mabel. Nick slaps his hands together violently in front of Mabel's face, and she goes into a trance. Nick holds her, frightened, and tells her he loves her. They all talk at her—"this is for your good [i.e., hospitalization]—you're sick and need it." They ignore her pleas to let her stay, to be with her children, to protect the children, and as a last resort to take her children with her. She snarls and gesticulates like a trapped wild animal, knowing she doesn't have a chance. The psychiatrist penetrates her with a hypodermic needle, and she is sedated and committed to a hospital.

Nick can't talk to his buddies about having hospitalized Mabel. He tries to stand in for her with the children, but he's not very tuned into them as children, nor as to what is appropriate for them. He screams at the kids' teacher at school; she backs off scared. He tells his kids, "I'm sorry I had to send your mother away. I'm sorry for everything."

Home from the Hospital—Six Months Later

Nick invites a crowd of friends and family to a party to celebrate Mabel's homecoming from the hospital. His mother, using the same shrill voice used to accuse Mabel six months earlier, tells him it is wrong for him to have invited all these people. He finally agrees she is right, but can't himself tell them to leave, asking his mother to do so.

Mabel arrives in the rain, escorted by her mother and father. She looks subdued and cautious. The doctor is there and advises her, *"Don't talk about the past."* She asks permission to see the children. Nick tells her to wait—"they'll cry … you'll get too emotional."

Her father out of the blue screams at Nick: "I will not stay for supper! All you ever serve is spaghetti. I hate spaghetti!" Mabel then snuggles into her father, sitting on his lap and kissing him. He reassures her in a warm and loving way. Nick watches, fearful and jealous. Her father also gets anxious and urges her to sit with her mother, saying "She needs you." But before this can happen, Nick grabs her and leads her upstairs, trying to connect with her, which he had not done spontaneously upon her arrival. "I love you. I'm with you; there's nothing you can do wrong. Just be yourself." He makes childish sounds, and asks her to play with him, "Give me a beh, beh." She is hesitant, and he urges, "Give me a real beh, beh." Here we see Nick encouraging her to be childish and playful with him, as they had been before the hospitalization.

At dinner they ask how it was for her in the hospital, but when she tells them about the daily shots and the shock treatments, and how awful it was for her, they shut her up, telling her, *"There's no sense talking about the past. Things will get better and better."*

Mabel says kindly and innocently, "I wish you'd all go home. Nick and I want to go to bed together." Someone says, "Not in front of the children." They ignore her request for privacy, not taking her seriously. She tries again, "Hello everyone. I wish you would all go home. Nick and I want to go to bed and talk." Again she is dismissed.

Someone says, "You're tired." She escalates in order to be recognized. She tells jokes. The children join in excitedly, and Nick screams, "end of jokes—end of conversations."

Chaos ensues. His mother takes a pot shot at Nick, "Look who's talking about conversation. He doesn't know how to put two words together." Mabel tries to talk seriously about her hospital experience, and Nick shouts "stop it, stop it." Mabel, feeling lonely and squashed by Nick, implores her father, "Dad will you stand up for me?" He, unable to understand what she's asking for, concretely interprets her request and stands up. Although her mother understands what Mabel is asking for, she only berates her husband, and gives Mabel nothing.

All is utter chaos. Mabel stands on the couch swaying and starts humming and gesticulating. Nick screams at her, "Get off the couch or I'll pull you down." Her father for one brief moment is outraged, yelling at Nick, "Leave my daughter alone, you!" but when Nick ignores him, and tells everyone to go, he leaves along with the others. One of the kids says, "Leave my mother alone." Nick threatens Mabel; she gets off the couch, gesticulates like a wild, trapped animal, and *runs into the bathroom.* Nick barges in; her hand is bleeding. Everyone is screaming. Mabel gets on the couch again and resumes her strange ballet. Nick screams, "If you don't get off the couch, I'll knock you down, and I don't want to do it." He slaps her in the face hard and knocks her down onto the floor. "I'll kill you," he screams. He tells the kids, "Your mother is all right. She's just resting here. Tell the kids you're just resting" and she obeys him, echoing his words.

They all go upstairs to put the kids to bed. Mabel, now calm, tells her daughter, "You know you look just like your father. You're Daddy's girl." Mabel then spends time with each son. The first says, "I'm worried about you, Mom." She says, "Don't worry about me. I'm a grown up." He tells her, "I love you, Mom," and she replies, "I believe that" and they kiss each other tenderly. She has a similar tender exchange of words and kisses with her second son. Nick is shown looking on apprehensive.

They are alone at last; Mabel now blames herself for all the chaos that occurred since she got home. "You know, I'm really nuts. I don't know how this whole thing got started. I think I just got tired you know." He cleans and bandages her cut. She asks, "Do you love me?" He looks at her, unable or unwilling to speak. She asks again, and he responds, "Let's clean up."

Discussion

This film exquisitely highlights domestic emotional and physical violence in the portraits of Mabel and Nick. Through the director's lens, the process or sequence of their marriage is dramatized with nightmarelike clarity. It is evident how naive and trusting Mabel is even when she instinctively knows better; how starved she is for love, acceptance, and recognition; and how terrified she is of abandonment. She is narcissistically vulnerable. She is passionate in her expressions of love and of hate. She turns to men as the source of strength, security, and gratification; and expects women to be withholding and rejecting. Mother was cold and inattentive; father was warm and supportive, but inadequate to protect her from her mother.

She tells her husband what she thinks are the five most important things: love, friendship, comfort, "I'm a good mother," and "I belong to you [Nick]." It is through her marriage to Nick that she hoped she would find the acceptance, recognition, support, and gratification that she was unable to get from her mother. It was through her marriage that she hoped to repair her damaged self and gain self-esteem as a woman. She is intensely animated, desperately longing to be seen, to be heard, to be validated.

She is unable to verbalize her anger at Nick, but gesticulates in a crazy, bizarre way, perhaps regressing to a preverbal experience of mother's lack of attunement. She believes it is her badness that causes him to act abusively. She tries very hard to be "nice" and nondemanding. She believes if she is not selfish, this will be the key to love and attachment (Katz, 1990). She unconsciously blames herself for her caregivers' parenting failures and for her husband's failures.

We see that she has been prepared by her parents for a kind of sadomasochistic dance with her husband. Her mother is frightened of her, and cold to her. Her father is loving, but concrete and passive—not able to understand or respond to his daughter's need for protection from mother or from abuse by Nick. Mabel adores and idolizes her father, clinging to him as a source of power, just as she clings to Nick.

Both her father and Nick oscillate between adoring and idealizing her, and rejecting, dismissing, and abandoning her. She reacts to what she is immediately presented with, not enlightened by both repeatedly disappointing her, nor able to reflect and appropriately protect herself.

Mabel doesn't trust her mother to competently care for either her children or herself. She expects that her mother will be oblivious to the pain of her children as she feels her mother was and still is dead to her pain. She unconsciously expects that the women walking on the street will be new editions of her mother, and as such would not give her the time she is asking for. Mabel's rage at her internalized bad mother and at her real mother are projected onto these women. She demonizes them, demanding the time rather than appropriately asking them for what she needs. She treats them as extensions of herself, not as separate people. When they self-protectively ignore her, she curses them. In this very brief scene, there is a clear enactment of a pathological mother/child relationship. Mabel expects to be deprived of her needs but feels addicted to depending on the frustrating mother. Her manner of trying to get her needs met alienates the person whom she hopes will nurture her. Her unconscious belief that no one will give her the "right time," that no one will tune into her and meet her needs, is validated.

Mabel desperately needs her children. They represent herself as a child and provide a chance for her to mother them and care for them in a way she was deprived of. She needs them to recognize, admire, love her in a way that her own mother was incapable of doing. She wants her children never to grow up. Then they will never abandon her; they are the only ones who forgive her when she's mean; they do not abuse her. Nonetheless she is attuned to their needs and is able to access her inner strength to do what's best for them. She is able to see them as separate. Likewise, she is intent on being recognized as a person in her own right—a person who is heard and whose privacy is respected. When Nick addresses her as "Ma," she is furious, both because she is more than a mother, and because she is not Nick's "Ma."

Nick loves Mabel, but when he feels overwhelmed and confused by her he defends himself by not listening or by calling her crazy. He loves his children but is unable to see them in terms of their own needs. He too has been deprived of good enough mothering, and longs for his wife to give him the acceptance and validation he did not get from his mother. He too is extremely vulnerable and fragile; is driven by impulse storms; thinks in childish, naive modes; and often acts on whim rather than with sound judgment. He quickly switches from love to hate, from compassion to anger and fear in relation to Mabel. For him, causes are external—"in the air." Desire is not within him nor within his lover; it is impersonal and mysterious. He is not an agent in his own life, but a victim of external forces and people.

He cannot reflect or understand that there are two worlds, two perspectives—his and hers. Bach (1994) discusses the ability to entertain multiple perspectives as a developmental achievement marking the transition from a primarily narcissistic orientation to an object-related one. This achievement results in a cohesive self in which good and bad parts are integrated and form part of the whole sense of oneself. Loved ones are also understood as whole persons who are both good and bad, loving and hating. Nick's inability to understand this is evidenced by his inability to deal with Mabel's anger without feeling totally trashed himself.

According to Bach (1994, p. 4) "sadomasochistic relations may be seen as a kind of denied or pathological mourning, a repetitive attempt to disclaim the loss or to repair it in fantasy, but an attempt that does not lead to resolution because in some dissociated part of the psyche that loss remains disavowed." In order to have an integrated sense of self and other, the past must be remembered. When there is no past, as well as no acknowledgment of loss, there is no mourning. Without mourning there is no forgiveness of self and other, and no mastery of loss (Klein, 1975; Loewald, 1980).

Nick is often unable to stay separate yet empathically attuned to either himself or Mabel, especially when she expresses strong feelings of love or hatred. In his conversation with his friend, Eddy, he expresses his love, sensitivity, and understanding of her at one moment, and at the next he abruptly distances himself from her and her feelings by cruelly judging her as crazy.

The couple react to each other both as parts of themselves and as new editions of old internal objects. They engage in a sadomasochistic dance, representing the past internalized drama between self and mother. They struggle to gain power, gratification, and autonomy by oscillating between submitting and withdrawing, between loving playfulness and hateful threats and punishments. Nick and Mabel play out, through projective identification, their past experiences with mother, and their inner scenarios of self-mother relationship, getting the other to alternate between being the abusive mother and the abused child. So, although they both desperately seek a more nurturing replacement of the mother within, they tragically repeat over and over again with each other the familiar destructive sadomasochistic patterns. Yet they both pretend "all is fine no matter what," reminiscent of Voltaire's *Candide*. As in *Candide*, disaster is inevitable; passive denial and projection result in escalating pain and suffering for both Mabel and Nick, as well as for the children.

When Mabel does try to physically and emotionally be close to Nick, he pushes her away, in many different ways. This is his attempt to regain control and shore up his own narcissistic need to be powerful. His inability to trust Mabel and feel safe with her has roots in his experience with his harshly controlling and demanding mother from whom he has not psychically separated. Nick is impulsive and given to externalization of his own motivations, desires, and fears. He tries to please his mother, yet she sometimes unexpectedly and viciously turns on him. He loves and hates her and transfers these split images onto his wife. He wants to be loved by Mabel, but cannot bear feeling vulnerable or guilty, emotions she frequently arouses in him. When she doesn't listen to him, he feels diminished and impotent, and at risk of being annihilated. When she doesn't submit to him but seeks the attention of other men (his co-workers, her father, her sons), he feels emasculated and becomes enraged. In both these situations, he loses control and attacks her emotionally and/or physically, thereby reaffirming his selfhood and masculinity.

Mabel's addictive inclination clues the viewer into her addictive relationship to Nick, an addiction representing a craving for what she has missed in her childhood. She craves for fulfillment from substances or persons who are seductively wonderful and promise she will experience herself as wonderful as well. These substances or people are used as substitutes for defective internalized self-soothing, self-screening, and self-regulating functions (Joseph, 1989; McDougall, 1995).

She creatively tries to protect, soothe, and enliven herself in other ways as well. Opera music is one way that she does this. It enlivens her, filling the emptiness within. The singing represents the emotionally attuned mother she never had, a mother alive to her. The song "Celeste Aida" moves her deeply. It is a tribute to a princess, Heavenly Aida, whose father passionately does "stand up" for his daughter, recognizing and supporting her as a woman. It is the essence of what she longs for and has never had. In addition, it is possible that opera music organizes her, temporarily quieting the chaotic "noises" and feelings inside her (Winnicott, 1971).

Mabel's punctuated visits to the bathroom, a room that is marked "PRIVATE", represent a safe retreat, a creative space which she uses to find herself, and to try to destroy the self she hates. It is perhaps an attempt to regress to an earlier stage, the anal stage, in which separation-individuation first occurs, along with the development of symbolization, mastery over loss, and the beginning awareness of self and other as whole, continuous people. She goes into the bathroom in order to regain a sense of control and balance, as well as a self she can live with.

Perhaps, most important, it is a man that she turns to in the hope of being heard, recognized, soothed, and enlivened. Mabel is desperate to be loved and admired. She longs to be empathically heard and recognized, instead the stranger, Garson Cross, wants her to recognize and gratify him, a repetition of her relationship with Nick and her mother. She renders herself defenseless through drink—a masochistic submission to the man. Although she fights when he tries to rape her, she is no match for him, and she is overtaken and raped. Her inability to face what has happened results in a delusion that this man is Nick, her husband. Garson takes no responsibility for his abuse of Mabel and her resulting delusional state. Mabel, as well as Nick, disavows. For example, the past events and experiences with Garson as well as with Nick are either disavowed or denied. She is unable to discuss her feelings about what had happened with either of them. The refrain Mabel hears inwardly and outwardly is, "Forget the past."

After the trauma of being stood up by Nick, raped by Garson Cross, and bombarded in the morning by Nick and his 12 buddies, she provokes and receives Nick's jealous rage. She then asks Nick to tell her what he wants her to be, and she'll be it. This is her manic defense warding off feelings of helplessness and worthlessness. Mabel doesn't have the appropriate internal signal anxiety to tune into danger and effectively deal with it, and because of this she is at times flooded with annihilation anxiety (Hurvich, 1989). Nor is she always able to tune into signals from others. And even when she senses she is on a disastrous course, she continues her addictive behavior, compulsively searching for her dream of realizing narcissistic comfort and self-esteem. She is naive and childlike in some ways, yet very nurturing and motherly in others. She is kind and gentle, empathizing with anyone among the guests whom she perceives as vulnerable or abused, teased or ridiculed.

Mabel doesn't allow herself to know consciously what she unconsciously knows; her facial and vocal expressions, body movements, gestures, and words are exquisitely eloquent. They are the signs of her abuse—not yet digested nor symbolized. Under stress, she emotes, unable to reflect and register. The crazy-making behavior by her husband is never acknowledged in the equation of her crazy behavior, and he is constantly switching his reactions to her. She allows herself to be talked out of her own experience by him.

The abuse of Mabel is not limited to her family. She also suffers at the hands of the psychiatrist, a mental-health professional who is manipulative and collusive. She doesn't trust him, but the moment he asks her for a drink, she transforms, becoming the gracious, fun-loving hostess, wanting to believe he wants to have fun with her, not hurt her. He carries out an agenda based on reports from Nick and Nick's mother. He prejudges Mabel, knowing her not at all. His treatment of her is at least as cruel and abusive as the rape.

Her unconscious fantasy that her mother doesn't cherish and understand her because she is a girl is revealed in her expectation that her own daughter will be daddy's girl. She remembers her mother's rejection of her choice of husband, in terms of "I know—you can't like him because he's not your son." I believe this can be translated to mean, "you can't like and recognize me because I'm not your son."

25

The oedipal implications of this are obvious, but I understand this as an oedipal rationalization for a preoedipal failure. Her passionate love of her father may then be seen as turning to father for the acceptance, recognition, and protection she lacked from mother.

Thus, although pre-oedipal issues are the primary sources of difficulty, oedipal themes also play a role in the portraits of Mabel and Nick. Mabel needs the attention, love, and recognition of men: Nick and strangers, her father and her sons. Nick becomes fearful and suspicious, even insanely jealous. He longs for his mother's love and admiration, but instead is spurned by her. His jealousy and narcissistic injury by mother result in sadistic control of Mabel. She then fragments, withdraws, and physically reacts with grimaces, noises, and gestures. He knows then that he has reached her. He is now again powerful and manly; he sees the emotional welts he has created. Now, feeling stronger, he tries to reassure her that she is good and has done nothing wrong. Mabel is also jealous and enraged by Nick's attachment to his mother, as well as to her mother, expressed in both instances nonverbally by grimaces, gestures, and sometimes noises.

Mabel cannot accept her own aggressive, hateful side. She has chosen a husband upon whom to project her own unacceptable parts. She provokes him to get angry; he then abuses her, and she can feel that she is the victim and enjoy the nobility of that position (Valenstein, 1973). She trusted him—they married because she was pregnant— and she naively believed and still believes he will give her what she wants and needs, even though he repeatedly disappoints her.

When the internal good mother is not well developed, as with Mabel, she then may know that she makes poor choices in her mate. Yet, there is something compelling about continuing the destructive pattern. In most cases the woman feels "if she just holds onto the old pattern a little longer, why surely the paradisiacal feeling she seeks will appear in the next heartbeat" (Estes, 1992).

Mabel's addictions to men, drinking, and smoking are unsuccessful efforts to nurture and comfort herself, to feel good, acceptable, and whole. She does not have a stable or clear sense of herself, her inner conflicts, or her feelings and thoughts. Much of the time she takes on the masochistic role of accepting abuse in order to maintain her attachment and avoid abandonment (Katz, 1990). The tyranny of silence or of condemnation (by her mother, Nick's mother, Nick, and the psychiatrist) leads her to fragment, make faces, gesticulate, mimic—all desperate attempts to find a self that is felt and responded to, not treated as invisible. When this fails, she tries to gain some sense of relief by cutting herself— a suicidal gesture. Through pain she can feel herself as someone. And through cutting or killing herself, she hopes to realize the unconscious fantasy of separating from and destroying the internal bad, destructive object—whether that be the "dead, unresponsive mother" (Green, 1986) or the "demon father-lover" (Kavaler-Adler, 1993). It is tragic that the psychiatrist was unaware of his own anxieties about women; he participates with Mabel's husband in an action rather than engaging in a reflection that could have helped. The husband's phallic mother and the psychiatrist protect the husband. It is Nick's fear of being engulfed and tyrannized by his mother that is projected onto Mabel; she then must be controlled. The fantasy shared by Nick, his mother, and the psychiatrist is that Mabel is the dangerous, feminine woman who could engulf and destroy. She must be put away.

REFERENCES

Bach, S. (1994). *The language of perversion and the language of love*. Northvale, NJ: Jason Aronson.

Estes, C. P. (1992). *Women who run with the wolves*. New York: Ballantine Books.

Filmmaker. (Fall, 1996). New York and Los Angeles: Karol Marlesko.

Green, A. (1986). The dead mother in *On private madness*. Connecticut: International Universities Press.

Hurvich, M. (1989). Traumatic moment, basic dangers and annihilation anxiety. *Psychoanal. Psychol.*, 6: 309-323.

Joseph, B. (1989). *Psychic equilibrium and psychic change in Addiction to near death*, M. Feldman & E. Bott Spillius, eds. London and New York: Routledge.

Kavaler-Adler, S. (1993). *The compulsion to create*. New York and London: Routledge.

Katz, A. (1990). Paradoxes of masochism. *Psychoanal. Psychol.*, 7 (2): 225-241.

Klein, M. (1975 [1930]). The importance of symbol-formation in the development of the ego. In *Love, Guilt and Reparation and Other Works—1921-1945*. London: Hogarth.

Loewald, H. (1980). Internalization, separation, mourning, and the superego. In *Papers on psychoanalysis*. New Haven and London: Yale University Press.

CHAPTER THREE ℘

Utz

Directed by George Sluizer (1992)

An earlier version of this study was presented on November 8, 2002, at the colloquium "Looking Out, Looking In: Cinema and Psychoanalysis," sponsored by the New York University Postdoctoral Program in Psychotherapy and Psychoanalysis.

Perversion, Fetish, and Creativity: The Fate of Desire in "Utz"

Honoreé de Balzac was a passionate collector who grew up in painful circumstances with a cold and rejecting mother. "Cut off already from all affection," he wrote, "I could love nothing, and Nature had made me loving! Is there an angel who collects the sighs of such ever-present feelings?" (Balzac, 1900).

George Sluizer's film *Utz*, based on the novella by Bruce Chatwin (1998), is a complex and poignant portrayal of another collector, another man whose lot it was to have had his loving nature thwarted by circumstance. *Utz* is a many-layered film, weaving psychological, political, and cultural issues into an intricate tapestry, but it is also the love story of two unusual people. Sluizer tells us very little about the histories of Baron Kaspar Joachim von Utz (played by Armin Mueller-Stahl) and the woman we know only as Marta (Brenda Fricker). His revelations are sparing and carefully timed. Nor does he give *Utz* much of a plot in the conventional sense. Yet he strikes chords that move the viewer deeply, perhaps more deeply than an ordinary narrative would have done. I focus in this study on how desire and longing—the "ever-present feelings" of Balzac's dilemma—live and move in the lives of Sluizer's subjects, and their fate in their world.

The Film / Introduction

A fabulous collection of antique Meissen porcelain figurines is the central image of this film, and it is a very rich image indeed.

Utz's collection attracts to itself the projections of all who see it. To Marius Fisher, an American antiques dealer (played by Peter Riegert), it means money. To the state museum in Prague it means the triumph of Communism over private ownership. To Utz's cynical old scientist friend Dr. Orlik (played by Paul Scofield) it means socks, and the countless other small conveniences he extorts from Fisher in exchange for hints on when the failing Utz might be willing to sell. But what do the figurines mean to Utz himself?

The engine of *Utz* is a mystery: Where is the priceless collection that Utz accumulated over the course of his life, protecting it successfully and at unknown cost first from the Nazis and then from the Communists? The answer to that second question is also the answer to the first: What did Utz's collection mean to him?

The film develops through a series of flashbacks and flash-forwards.

1 Utz (played by Armin Mueller-Stahl) is an elegant, driven, shy man. He is half-Jewish, born to wealth and privilege on a grand estate near the Meissen porcelain works. We learn that his father died when he was young; his mother is never mentioned. Somehow—we are not privy to the details—he has managed to preserve his life and his wealth through the political storms that ravaged mid-twentieth century Europe. When the film begins, however, he is an elderly man living with his collection in a rundown apartment house in Prague.

We first see Utz at a porcelain auction. His aggressive bidding defeats the dealer Fisher, who marvels at the exorbitant price he is willing to pay for a figurine. Utz explains that he must have this piece, since it will complete his set of all twenty-one Meissen monkey musicians; "I'm sure you understand," he tells Fisher. Fisher does not, and neither do we, at least not yet. This movie is a carefully constructed mosaic. Each piece adds to a cumulative portrait of Utz, his inner life, and the place of his collection within it, and each indirectly addresses the puzzle of the vanished collection.

After the auction, Utz returns to his hotel room. He unwraps his new acquisition and takes it to the window to study it. A musical leitmotif in a minor key is heard for the first time. The music, and the sound of a woman's voice calling, joins this scene with the next, in which we see Utz as a child, entranced by a bowl of vigorous tadpoles that he is holding up close to his face. When he hears his name being called, he tears himself away, awkwardly crossing the empty expanses of garden and the deserted entry halls of the house on his scooter. Ignoring his grandmother's worried admonitions, he zooms past her toward another "fishbowl"—a vitrine full of Meissen figurines. There he stops, points to the porcelain figure of a harlequin within, and declares passionately, "I want that."

"No," says his grandmother firmly. "Perhaps one day. It belongs to your father." The haunting music returns.

Back in the present, we see Utz as an older man struggling along a shabby street and up the three flights of stairs to his apartment. When he opens the door from the dim hallway, an astonishing vision greets our eyes: hundreds of figurines illuminated in mirrored etagères. For a few moments he gazes at them, and we see his own face reflected behind them, as though he were one of them. Then he collapses.

The next scene is the funeral of Utz's father when the boy is around ten. The musical leitmotif is heard again, and it returns immediately afterward, when Kaspar's grandmother gives him the coveted harlequin. Both the theme and the statue seem to denote longing and desire.

2 Utz is a very young man when his grandmother dies, leaving him her fortune. His passion for Meissen blooms, and he begins to study it devotedly. The musical theme returns as we see him alone on his vast and magnificent, but empty, estate.

Next, in disconcerting contrast, the middle-aged Utz is at dinner in a Prague restaurant with Orlik, his best friend, and the dealer Fisher. They order trout and are told that there is none, even though they can plainly see several trout swimming in a tank just behind them. Now, however, Utz is no longer lord of the manor. *Those* trout, the waiter nervously whispers, are being saved for the Party members at the next table; for Utz and his friends, they do not exist. They will have to content themselves with carp, spelled on the menu "crap." Fisher and Orlik can laugh at this error, but Utz cannot; he is going to have to eat shit, and he is powerless to change his fate. The camera cuts from a close-up of the men sitting at the table to a long shot of the dining room, shrinking them until they are small figures in their sparkling surround. No longer the owner of grandeur, the director seems to be telling us, Utz is now owned himself, a prisoner in a showcase that belongs to others.

Utz's apartment is invaded by officials of the state museum. They have come to catalog his collection, which must go to the museum when he dies. They are unappreciative and careless, and they break one of the pieces. Their heedlessness drives Utz to an agonized shriek: *"Be careful!"* Enraged by accumulated indignities and thinking of leaving Prague for good, he arranges a trip to a luxurious spa in Switzerland. Before he goes, he tells his servant to set the table for two; it is she who will be his guest that evening. In a close-up, her middle-aged face is wistful and serene.

Now attention turns to the servant, Marta (played by Brenda Fricker). We see her as a beautiful young woman living on the farm where she raises geese. She lies on the grass sighing in delight as one bird, with whom she has a very loving relationship, nuzzles her face and ruffles her hair with its bill. In another idyllic and sensual scene, she swims naked in the river, her goose swimming along beside her. But a horde of village men have been spying on her, and as she sets out for home, they chase her, armed with pitchforks and sticks. A passing car (Utz's) spontaneously stops and lets her in.

Flashing forward again, we see Utz at the spa. Here, too, he is frustrated. Here is yet another restaurant where he sees what he wants but cannot get it; the waiter pays no attention to him. The elegant women he awkwardly approaches look right through him, ignoring or disdaining his timid smiles. We hear the music of longing again as the aristocratic objects of his desire turn their attentions elsewhere. He sees other guests being waited on, other men kissing their sweethearts. He can observe and he can want, but he cannot participate. He decides not to join the bathers in the public pools, and retreats to his room. In his lonely bath, he recalls a day in the country

32

hunting mushrooms with Marta. He finds a wonderful one. He triumphantly holds it up, and she responds with pleasure and excitement. He decides to go home.

Back in Prague, the antique dealer Fisher visits Utz. Rats are foraging in the vestibule of his building when they enter, but Utz doesn't notice them. His attention is focused on the magical world upstairs. Fisher is stunned by the contrast between the splendor of the illuminated and mirrored display inside the apartment and the squalor below. How did this magic come to be?

"History was on my side," says Utz. "In the thirties it was Jews escaping from the Nazis, and later the aristocrats escaping the communist regime. They had excellent pieces of porcelain and needed money." The musical leitmotif returns. As Fisher watches, Marta lights a candelabrum and places it on the dining table. Utz puts an opera recording on the phonograph, and then takes out several small figures of aristocratic men and women, tentatively moving them together and apart to the glorious music of a soprano voice. Marta sits behind him smiling as Utz's expression becomes increasingly rapt. Finally, at the ecstatic peak of the aria, he selects two figures, a man and a woman carrying a child, and joins them in a harmonious dance. This is a climactic scene of shimmering sensuality and passionate sexual intensity.

In the following scene, Utz and Fisher are in Prague's ancient Jewish cemetery, where Rabbi Loew, creator of the notorious *golem* of Jewish folklore, is buried. Utz tells the story: The rabbi wanted a servant to whom he would not have to pay wages, and in a hubristic imitation of God, he fashioned a mess of clay into the likeness of a human and gave it life and power. One day the *golem*—a Hebrew word meaning unformed clay—went berserk, tearing up trees and houses until its creator had to destroy it. Is Utz saying that the porcelain figures are alive? Fisher asks, and Utz answers, "I am, and I'm not…. They die in fire and they come to life again." He offers a personal manifesto: "A man-made figure is a blasphemy and collecting is a form of idolatry. We Jews, and I call myself a Jew, make the best collectors because it's sinful—because it's dangerous!'"

In another flashback, the Communist state decrees that single men must move into dormitories. Utz marries Marta, and so is permitted to remain in the three-room apartment that houses his collection. After the formal ceremony, Marta, in a white dress and veil, kisses Utz on the forehead.

The music that accompanies Utz's play with the figurines, the "Song to the Moon" from Dvorak's opera *Rusalka*, takes on a deeper meaning when we learn in the next scene that Utz has a second obsession: opera singers. At first, Fisher is startled to discover pictures of famous sopranos festooning Utz's bathroom, their extravagant costumes hanging on the wall. Then, the camera shows us Utz at the opera, listening to their voices and focusing his gaze on their singing mouths, which are at the same time both fascinating and menacing. One singer tells Fisher, "He fell in love with my voice." He courts divas, inviting them for a stylized and romantic evening of dinner, dancing, and bed. But he rejects them soon after, becoming dismissive and contemptuous. Marta is jealous of these women. Cleaning up in the kitchen while Utz is dancing with one (in a style reminiscent of the dance he executes with the figurines), she deliberately smashes a dish; this is the first evidence of her rage, and a foreshadowing of what is to come. When we next see her, she is alone with Orlik at Utz's funeral, where she announces with satisfaction that no one else is there because she sent all the discarded lovers to the wrong church.

Flashing backward once more, we see Utz on his deathbed, paralyzed. He signals with eye movements to Marta that he wants his collection destroyed. Aware that he is watching, she breaks the pieces one by one on a glass table, starting with the harlequin that had belonged to his father, and she helps him to drop one of the figurines himself. In this second climactic scene, Utz is once again ecstatic and powerful. And this time Marta too is ecstatic and powerful, laughing with pleasure as she shatters the fragile figurines one after another. The recurrent "porcelain" leitmotif is heard for the last time.

After Utz's death, Fisher and the museum officials seek the collection. Fisher goes back to the village of Marta's youth, to which she has retreated, but she eludes him. She keeps faith with Utz and with their secret.

Discussion

But what *is* their secret? What are we to "understand," as Utz put it to Fisher, from this story? As I have said, we know little about Utz. He has suffered great reverses in his life, and great danger and fear. He has the means to live anywhere, but he remains in depressed and despised Prague. He is obsessed with women but has no enduring sexual relationships. Only his passion for the figurines never flags. It is renewed over and over again as he acquires them, protects them, manipulates them, and eventually destroys them.

Two intertwining musical images weave through the film. The first is the delicate and wistful "porcelain" leitmotif that is Sluizer's commentary on Utz's moments of desire and longing; the second is the ecstatic love song from a Czech opera that Utz himself chooses to accompany his dramatic ritual of consummation with the Meissen figures. This musical link between the two collections (of porcelain and of women) makes clear that the first is not exempt from the passion more concretely realized in the second, and that collecting is for Utz an activity that both expresses and contains intense feeling.

With these little statues Utz creates, over and over, dramas that excite, enliven, and delight him. One after another he stages stately masques in a world over which he exercises absolute control. The same quality of repetitive enactment of a compelling fantasy, and the need for total control over it, appears in his ritualized courtship and abandonment of singers. Utz's collections are his avenue to the world of desire and passion, a world that he keeps starkly, although at times unhappily, at arm's length in his "everyday" interpersonal life.

The ritualized repetition that Utz displays in his drama with the figurines and his stylized seductions of singers is characteristic of the particular adjustment to a dangerous inner (and outer) world that is usually called *perversion*. His use for erotic ends of inanimate objects (porcelain figurines, opera costumes) or parts of animate objects (the singing voice, the open mouth) is characteristic of the particular erotic behavior usually called *fetish.*

Perversion and *fetish* are words that evoke intense feelings in the world at large with equal measures of fascination and disgust.

3 Psychoanalysts have theorized about these concepts in ways both overlapping and widely divergent. While most writers agree that perversion and fetish depend on substitution—of part for whole, of nonhuman for human, of inanimate for animate, as Stoller (1985) puts it, observational studies of the way such substitutions are integrated into ordinary lives are rare. Stoller has done some important work in this field, but his work on this aspect of perversion has so far attracted little attention. He recognized erotic fetishism as "containing in its structure mechanisms of defense that are central for understanding all human relationships" (p.121) and went on to make a telling and characteristic point: "The capacity to substitute ... helps make life bearable—even enjoyable—when intimacy, insight, and lovingness would be too intense" (p. 121).

Stoller's resistance to reductionism, his attention to detail, and his capacity to remain emotionally close even to sometimes very distancing behavior, gave him a uniquely humane view of what he called "the erotic imagination." Sluizer shares Stoller's gift for "naturalistic observation" (Stoller, 1985, pp. 1-9), and in his film he gives perversion a human face. In this tradition, my goal here is not to engage in the controversies over the etiology of perversion and fetishism, but to delineate, in an exploration of Utz's life and passions, *how* perversion may "make life bearable"—and how Utz's collection served for him as the "angel" of which Balzac spoke with such longing.

It goes without saying, I hope, that this discussion is a commentary on only one facet of the immensely complex and multi-faceted organization that is a human being. In fact, my point is precisely that Baron Kaspar Joachim von Utz is *not* a one-dimensional caricature of a man who can be defined by any given aspect of his emotional repertoire. He participates in all the intra-psychic, interpersonal, and existential (political, cultural, social, etc.) dimensions of the human sphere. As I understand it, and as I will try to explicate, a neurotic condition of perversion can and does exist simultaneously with other dynamics. Utz's perverse characteristics are one aspect of his personality, but not the only one.

Perversion

There are many views of perversion, reflecting, as I see it, the likelihood that perversion is not one discrete psychological organization. In this study I take the view that perversion is a compromise between defense and enactment, one way of externalizing the strain of simultaneous love and rage when such contradictory feelings cannot be altogether accepted and contained intra-psychically. Many such balances between defense and enactment may be enshrined in the ritualistic substitutions of perversion and fetish.

Perversion finesses the problem of ambivalence by substitution (of a symbolic love object for a more vulnerable or more dangerous real one) and by ritualized drama, both of which interpose emotional distance between subject and object, and so keep both parties "safe" at times of intense feeling. It is a compromise formation, and like all compromise formations it has two faces. It permits gratification of desirous feelings and discharge of angry ones where that would otherwise not be possible, yet in the very distancing that affords safety, it defends against more immediate and intimate connections with the beloved object. The contour of this compromise is the landscape that Sluizer paints so masterfully in *Utz*.

A Very Brief Comment on Perversion in Psychoanalysis

Freud related perversion in various ways to conflicts between the desire for sexual pleasure and the fear of punishment. He (1905) felt that perversion is the "negative" of neurosis in that neuroses *inhibit* pleasure in their manner of dealing with internal conflict (through repression and symptom formation), whereas perversions are a creative way of achieving pleasure *in spite of* unconscious fears of retribution or loss. His understanding roughly was that there were two means by which the imagined threat could be held at bay, thereby allowing sexual pleasure to be pursued in safety. The first was through the guilt-assuaging acceptance of a lesser (symbolic or actual) punishment—a sadomasochistic solution (Freud, 1919). The second was through the magical use of a fetish (1927 and see the next section).

Since Freud, psychoanalytic writers have understood perversion in many different ways, among them (and this is a very small sample) seeing perversion (1) as defensive sexual behavior in the face of narcissistic insult or deficit (Goldberg, 1975); (2) as a denial of differences, both generational and gender, resulting in anal sadism (1978); or (3) as a normal development that is retained (Chasseguet-Smirgel, in *all* individuals in order for the sexual passions to remain alive (Marucco, 1997). Most writers (for example Khan, 1979, and Nersessian, 1998) take quite a dark view of perverse psychopathology, which they tend to see as "deeper" than neurosis—unconflictual, fueled by destructiveness rather than sexuality, and with intractable acting-out as the inevitable result. Stoller (1985), however, explicitly challenges Freud's long-accepted separation between perversion and neurosis: "I do not believe that neurosis is the negative of perversion—I believe, rather, that perversion is an erotic neurosis" (p. 134).

4 Dimen (2001) objects to the very concept, on the grounds that it is pejorative and without clinical usefulness.

My own view inclines toward Stoller's end of the spectrum. There are many ways of keeping passion and desire alive; some of these include perversion or fetish, and these are distinct *in some ways* from those that do not. The point made by Dimen (2001) and her colleagues about the need to avoid pathologizing is a valid one, and Stoller's naturalistic approach seems to me exemplary in that regard. But the naturalistic approach is not often elaborated in the *clinical* psychoanalytic literature. Its realization in the persons of Utz and Marta made visible to me Stoller's concept of an erotic neurosis and the many forms it takes within ordinary lives.

Fetish

The American Heritage Dictionary (third edition) defines a fetish as (1) "An object that is believed to have magic or spiritual powers," or (2) "an object of unreasonably excessive attention or reverence." Psychoanalytic writers have come to more diverse understandings of what a fetish represents and what its latent meanings and functions are; like perversion, this diversity reflects the complexity of the subject. However, most analysts, beginning with Freud, see the use of fetish as a way of simultaneously fulfilling desire while magically defending against the unconscious belief that such fulfillment will result in intolerable destruction or loss.

A fetish may be either a thing or a part or aspect of a person—a shoe, for example, or a foot or a voice. It is an *enduring* substitute for the object whose loss is feared, a substitute that can withstand whatever passions are directed toward it and in its persistence "prove" the immunity of the object to destruction. (One such scenario is Freud's [1927] view that the fetish was a penis equivalent, which by its very presence assuaged the fear of castration, leaving the anxious male free to pursue his pleasures with a woman). A fetish is also controllable as no real complete other person, in all his or her complexity and difference, can ever be; thus the frequent conjunction of fetish and sadomasochism. In this scenario, the magic of the fetish allows for the disavowal of the threatening separateness—physical and psychic—between the self and the desired object that make loss and disappointment inevitable. It permits the illusion of self and other as a perfect unity that no passion can sunder. Because the compromise formations of perversion are so often accomplished by the use of such idealized, externalized, and indestructible objects, fetish is often associated with perversion, although it need not be.

In yet another scenario, the fetish is seen as a defense against sadistic destruction of love objects, both internal and external. Payne (1939), following Klein (1946) and echoed later by Stewart (1970) and Bach (1994), pioneered the view that a person feeling threatened by his or her own overwhelming aggression may seek reinforcement against it in the magical form of the fetish.

Stoller (1985) points out that the fetish may be a *representation* of the longed-for other, or aspects of her, such as her breast, her skin, or her voice (pp. 131-131). He emphasizes that a fetish can be not only a means of access to an erotic object, but also an erotically exciting and/or soothing object in itself—porcelain, smooth as a mother's skin, for example, or the strains of a heavenly female voice, may provide blissful entrée into merger with a desired object. In *Utz*, we see both of these uses of fetish. The porcelain figurines are objects of erotic desire in themselves to Utz; the mouths, voices, and appurtenances of the singers arouse him, and allow him to experience and satisfy, if briefly, *sexual* desire.

5 Scenarios like these are representative, but not comprehensive, examples of the many psychoanalytic views of fetish that have flourished over the years. They are sketches of common psychological themes that come up for many people under widely varying circumstances. For this reason, I disagree with Nersessian's (1998) view that fetishistic behavior indicates "serious pathology"— it may, but I think it more accurate to consider the use of fetish a psychological technique that can be used across the entire spectrum of psychopathology. I do concur with the school of thought that sees in fetish a way of handling sadistic impulses, but here, too, I hesitate to make assumptions about any implied depth of pathology. Sadistic impulses in themselves are not pathological. Indeed, they are both universal and indispensable; they are necessary drivers of such important aggressive phenomena as vitality, curiosity, and the ability to compete. Certainly they can be frightening, but occasional recourse to magical reinforcement against them (like walking very carefully on a pavement—"Step on a crack, break your mother's back") is very common and not particularly ominous in itself. As Bach (1994) points out, the necessary developmental task for all of us is to find the point of balance from which we can enjoy the excitement of action and fantasy without risking the loss or destruction of other or of self. A little magic can sometimes help in this task. It is when we *fail* to find that point of balance that perversion, or the use of fetish, becomes dangerous.

The psychoanalytic ideas about perversion and fetish that have proliferated over the last hundred years illuminate many facets of these deep and puzzling psychological developments. But the film *Utz*, as a work of art so often can, illuminates the experience of a *person*—not one facet or another, but a whole person, struggling within the conditions of his life to maintain his vitality in the best way he can. While perverse fantasies and behavior may be dramatic, criminal, or even deadly, lesser degrees of perverse preoccupation are extremely common—some psychoanalytic writers feel they are universal—and they may be subtle, private, and relatively benign. For every sadistic murderer, there are dozens of movies about sadistic murders and millions of people who enjoy watching them.

6 Such interests may be ways of enjoying severely destructive and sadistic impulses while defending against enacting them in the pursuit of passion. In other words, perversions may be ways of enabling desirous *and aggressive* release, both of which are necessary for erotic vitality. Depending upon the balance between loving and hateful passions in any given person, the perversion will be weighted more to one or the other. In Sluizer's *The Vanishing* (see no. 6), the murderous passions win out; in Utz, the loving passions are stronger. Perversions may take many forms, but they have in common a quality of enactment; they are stylized, ritualized, repetitive dramas compulsively played out by individuals (male or female) to engage their passions when other ways are foreclosed or seem too dangerous. *Utz* calls our attention back to Freud's early, normative, and nonjudgmental view that perversion is one of the many creative ways by which human beings muddle through the demands of their lives (Freud, 1905).

The Fate of Desire in Utz

Utz collects porcelain and women. It seems clear that aspects of his collecting behavior are characteristic of both fetishism and perversion. Collecting is by no means always a manifestation of perversion, nor is a collection necessarily a fetish. However, identification of the perverse organization that underlies *this particular* collector's behavior allows a fuller understanding both of Utz himself and of his curious asymmetrical relationship with Marta.

In his collecting he is sure that his love objects are in his control, whether they be Meissen figurines, his one-night divas, or his servant.

7 The drive to acquire and reject, to court and dismiss—whether in the auction house, the opera house, or his own home—all these allow for some play of both his desirous and his sadistic impulses, and in so doing release the pressure to act upon them in more threatening ways. His perverse compromise protects him, allowing him to experience sexual and aggressive passion, but also to avoid the kind of loving erotic engagement with a truly separate other in which disappointment and risk, and the rage they evoke, are inevitable.

We don't know enough about Utz and Marta to speculate responsibly about their early relationships with their parents. We do know that they are lonely people. Utz lost his father early. We learn nothing at all about his mother, and the only childhood caregiving figure we see is the serious and anxious grandmother in her starched white coat. Even as a child Utz seems detached from her; his passions are directed to dramas enacted behind glass or on stage. The vigor of the tadpoles and the more highly elaborated, if less lively, world of his father's Meissen figurines, the grandeur of the opera—these offer dramatic scenarios of passion, but no real people to love. In the film Marta as a young woman is shown alone, accompanied only by the beloved goose with whom she expresses and enjoys both love and sensuality. We do see clearly, that as adults, Utz and Marta have a strong and loving attachment—but an eccentric and asexual one, the limitations of which allow both to avoid the dangers posed by an intimate erotic relationship.

As Sluizer suggests repeatedly, Utz is a man of great sensuality. We see that Marta is a sensual woman in her reactions to the goose and to the wild mushroom. She has made a life without passionate sexual relationship. We do not know exactly why, but we are given a powerful clue in one terrifying view of the violent and rageful men of her village, who, convinced that she has taken her pet goose as a lover, label her a witch and enact an extremely threatening vision of outraged adult sexuality. Marta has her own terrors, and so can respect Utz's. He concentrates on his porcelain, and she, after losing the goose in her escape, concentrates on him.

They are both, in their quiet ways, bitter and oppositional. Prague suits Utz's "melancholy temperament," he says, and so he remains there, his passions carefully compartmentalized, complying (superficially) with the communist authorities. His friend Orlik criticizes him for this, but in fact Utz is a secret rebel, and in his conversation with Fisher in the cemetery he makes clear how much he enjoys the angry power of breaking the rules. (Etchegoyen, 1978, discusses at length the pleasure in rule breaking that he feels is characteristic of the perverse transference.)

Utz is not the patsy that Orlik implies, and he has a rapacious side. Even as he himself struggled to survive the Nazis and the Communist takeover, he was taking advantage, he tells us directly, of the misfortunes of others to build his extravagant collection.

But Utz is aware that his rule breaking and his preference for personae over people are as dangerous as they are seductive. He points out the fine line between a person and a construction—"Adam [also a notorious rule-breaker] was not only the first human being, but also the first ceramic sculpture"—and he goes on to consider the antisocial aspects of the *golem*, another sculpture ambivalently celebrated in Jewish folklore, who comes to life, and to disobedience, with catastrophic consequences. "A man-made figure," Utz makes clear, "is a blasphemy." This view of the *golem*[8] and its enactment of its master's projected rage hints that Utz's passionate attachment to his own clay idols contains more than a little fury.

Underneath her obedience, Marta too harbors a secret defiance. Her refusal to make herself sexually available in the expected way evokes the sadistic rage of the men of her village (and may, in fact, have originated in response to the brutality of their sexuality). During one of Utz's staged seductions, she gives a hint of her own usually suppressed rage by smashing a plate in the kitchen. Sluizer gives us a hint as well, with a split-second glimpse of an ominous cast projected onto one of the figurines. Thus the director links Marta as well as Utz to the ambivalently charged collection of porcelain, and makes it, explicitly, for both of them, a symbol of rage as well as of love. Later, Marta delights in thwarting his ex-lovers' wishes to either visit him when he is dying, or to attend his funeral.

Utz and Marta are joined by Utz's facilitation of Marta's sexual compromise—the sadomasochistic constellation of jealous desire, voyeuristic excitement, and rage that they enact in the safety of their home every time he trysts with one of his singers. They are joined, as well, in his ritual play with the porcelain figurines, which she facilitates and enjoys by lighting the candelabra and playing an aria from *Rusalka*; these enactments are *their* trysts.[9] Utz and Marta's perverse alliance with each other is established through the medium of Utz's collection(s) and their complex and interdependent desires, fears, and loves.

The director takes pains to show us that this is no happenstance. There is a dynamic compromise here. It contains (in that word's twin senses of inclusion and control) love and hate, beauty and pain, and it serves them both well. Although Utz and Marta are married, he does not bed her, Orlik explains to Fisher. But when Fisher expresses sympathy, Orlik is matter-of-fact. "It is not sad. She loves him." And he loves her. They are devoted to each other. They understand and protect each other; they long for each other when separated; they facilitate the fulfillment of each other's needs and desires; they assuage for each other the feeling of alienation that haunts them. But their committed love, their sadomasochistic bargain, serves at the same time to *defend* against the physical, passionate, bodily love that can take over the self and threaten its temporary loss in ecstatic penetration of and merger with the other.

Neither Utz nor Marta can experience passion comfortably in the unpredictable relationships that occur with complex, whole other people. When she gives him his legacy from his father, Utz's grandmother tells him that porcelain with its skin-smooth surface meant phallic potency, beauty, and immortality to the ancient Chinese. Porcelain serves for Utz as a connection with both father and mother, which in its perfection and its lack of sovereignty disavows the risk of pain, loss, and danger.

Utz is bold and confident in his desire for Meissen, and aggressive in pursuing it. He is equally aggressive in his pursuit of his singers. But when, as at the spa, he must deal with a real woman rather than a persona or a statue, he is capable only of timid and awkward approaches that end repeatedly in failure and rejection. He can love only an idealized or an idealizing woman; once he beds her, desire is transformed into hatred and disgust. As Utz says cruelly of one of his discarded lovers: "She's mad. She was a famous soprano, but a crazy person."

In his need for a magical talisman that will protect and enliven him, Utz searches compulsively for yet another figurine, yet another diva. Werner Muensterberger (1994), a psychoanalyst who has made an extensive study of collecting and collectors, has observed that obsessive collecting can be enlisted in the service of binding anxiety and tolerating affect. In his words, "Favoring things instead of people may be one of several solutions for dealing with emotions that echo old traumata and uncertainties.... Affection becomes attached to things, which in the eyes of the beholder can become animatized, like the amulets and fetishes of preliterate humankind or the holy relics of the religionist" (p. 9).10 This view helps us to understand the role that Utz's collection plays in his psychology; so, perhaps, does Freud's comment that "every collector is a substitute for a Don Juan Tenorio, and so, too, is the mountaineer, the sportsman, and such people. These are erotic equivalents." (Freud, 1886-1889, p. 209).11

The Disappearance

We can speculate that Utz has found both an evocative substitute for the absent loving securities of his childhood, and an outlet for the healthy aggressiveness that frightening personal and political circumstances required him to displace. To explain the mystery of the collection's disappearance, we can return to Payne's (1939) hypothesis that fetishistic eroticism contains and defends against terrifying sadistic fantasies.

When Utz tells Fisher that porcelain "dies by fire and comes to life by fire," we wonder whether this is not his own experience in the furnaces of Eros—the fire that brings us to life, but at the same time awakens the burning disappointments and rages that threaten to destroy the self or the beloved other. Erotic passions also threaten to enslave and take over the loving, dependent self, leaving it open to rejection and abandonment. Underneath his melancholy, Utz is an angry and vulnerable man, and afraid to get too close to the fire for which he longs.

In his comment to Fisher about his collecting ("It's sinful. It's dangerous."), he acknowledges his view of passion as dangerous, and once again (as in the restaurant) we see the aggressive pride that drives him, and the anger and defiance that make him fear his own destructiveness—the Rabbi Loew, the *golem*, in himself. He is engaged in a personal war with God, but he fears God's retaliation, and so resorts to indirect means of waging war, as he resorts to indirect means of making love. Much as the beginning of an analytic session may clue us into the themes that will develop within it, the opening images of this movie—the auction, the tadpoles, the harlequin—subtly show us the themes and underlying issues in the protagonist's life. He was a child of a passionate and determined nature living in conditions certainly of great danger and probably of real deprivation. His home was a place of beauty but also emptiness, peopled only by himself and a reserved and worried grandmother who rarely touches him physically, but whom we see deeply engaged with him when she gives him the harlequin, and later when she instructs him on the wonders of porcelain. It is in the world of this beautiful and magical substance, which has come to him through his father and through his inheritance from his father's mother, that he longs to live.

Utz's collection is the organizing principle in his life. It keeps him vital and alive, powerful and creative, purposeful and envied. It gives his life color and power in the bureaucratic greyness of Prague, and a venue in the wider world where he can admire and be admired. It allows him aggressive release—for example, in the foiling of Fisher at the auction and again upon his death. The contrast between Utz's oppressed life in communist Czechoslovakia and the magical world of his Meissen figurines—between his painful awareness of alienation and his omnipotent fantasy of pleasure and delight—are brilliantly portrayed in back-and-forth sequences in this film.

But as we move through the film, Sluizer makes clear that Utz's delicate balance is threatened. First, he learns that the figurines are not his to keep; upon his death they will become the property of the state. This violates his omnipotence and his identity, and for the first time we see him openly enraged. The meaning of the collection continues to evolve even while Utz is on his deathbed, as Sluizer focuses increasingly less on its beauty and more on its threatening potential. The intimations of destruction in the scene in the cemetery become reality.

Indeed, even the look of the figurines evolves. Utz once tells Fisher that Kendler, the maker of his harlequin, was not only the finest of the Meissen sculptors, but also a great satirist. But the ironic quality that he once prized as a delightful manifestation of an artist's skill loses its charm. The director's portrayal of the collection takes on a shockingly different cast, corresponding to the interior change in Utz as death approaches. The lovely little figures now look ugly and menacing, similar to how we saw them previously through the eyes of Marta in her jealous rage. They have not, after all, been able to protect Utz from loss and fear. Their paralysis now mocks his own. Undying themselves, they derisively taunt his ephemeral humanity. As Utz's thoughts turn darkly toward his end, their magic becomes black magic; now when he looks at them, he grimaces and moans. He and Marta are alone now, and he himself is a figurine, a helpless object dependent on her manipulations.

Klein (1946) might suggest that Utz's preoccupation with perfect porcelain and his serial idealizations and devaluations of opera goddesses are a defensive form of psychological splitting that is now beginning to break down. Keeping love and rage separate has protected his freedom to desire by containing fears that the imminence of death is finally making irrelevant. Payne would argue that now that Utz is totally paralyzed he is finally free to acknowledge and honor his *wish* to destroy what he loves, that he no longer needs a fetish to contain and control the terrifying conjunction of loving and sadistic impulses that he has repressed for so long. Kohut (1984) might think that the pain of the sudden failure of this heretofore reliable self-object—which in fact can ensure neither potency nor immortality—evokes in Utz an uncontrollable outburst of narcissistic rage.

In any case, Utz's final desire is for an act of impassioned destruction. His fury, long repressed and turned inward into melancholy, is finally given its due in full and explosive expression. In dying, Utz can

47

finally unleash the power that might, if he had feared it less, have allowed him fuller and more vibrant relationships in life.

Utz's final act of will is carried out by Marta, who joins in it readily. His impending death has released her as well from Rusalka's fate—the risk of destroying the beloved object. Free now to live their rage, he and she achieve a new merger in their triumphant joy in destruction, an ecstatic *petite mort* in the face of the Grim Reaper himself, a shattering of Marta's long-sequestered virginity. As the small porcelain figures crash and splinter on a glass table, Utz and Marta become one at last in orgiastic consummation.

This final cataclysm gives Utz intense pleasure and a final surge of vitality. We hear for the last time the theme that accompanied the child's declaration of desire for his father's harlequin as Marta smashes the priceless collection piece by piece, beginning with the harlequin itself. But now the noise of the porcelain breaking makes a visceral counterpoint to the delicate melody, a percussive background that gives substance and vigor to the wistful music of his life. His passions, freed, can blossom in the warmth of his fury. Eros and Thanatos have found each other at last.

In summary, Utz and Marta are living intra-psychic lives in which love, rage, and sexuality are rigorously compartmentalized, in which there has been a failure to achieve, the union of tenderness and lust (Richards, 2003, p. 1200). Yet these passions remain available to them in forms that can be called fetishistic and perverse, as their established rituals both defend against the dangers of overwhelming wishes for loving or sadistic merger and provide opportunities for gratifying them safely.

This movie illustrates, intimately and vividly, how the perverse compromise can protect and enable passion when the powerful ambivalences of erotic love are too overwhelming to be risked, and when fear of engaging them might otherwise result in the psychic death of depression or schizoid withdrawal. *Utz* portrays the use of the perverse compromise as a comfort and a connection in the lives of two people who have not been fortunate enough to develop a robust and unfettered capacity to tolerate the simultaneous fires of love and rage. It reminds us that like any other compromise formation,

48

perversion may be a creative response (unconsciously devised) to the complexities of psychological life and relationship.

I value this portrayal because it challenges our tendency to be too monolithic and negative in our view of perversion. There is no invariable association between perversion and crime or evil, and it is not necessarily true that the pleasures of perversion are so great that perverse people are not motivated to analyze or relinquish them. In my clinical experience, and contrary to much received wisdom, perversion is *not* always ego-syntonic (see Goldberg, 1975; Klein, 1927; Stein, 2003). That is, some people are inclined to analyze and relinquish it. *Utz* illustrates perversion and fetish as an adaptive and sometimes oddly dignified defense of self and passion in the face of the human condition, which unfortunately is inseparable from fear, loss, and pain.

This capacity of the artist to expand a viewer's grasp of the human situation is one of the reasons that the arts are such a rich field for psychoanalytic study. Repeated viewings of this film have opened me to the reality of varying gradations and kinds of perversion, and to the value as well as the pain for the individual in this type of compromise formation. It has also enabled me to contemplate the perverse dilemma with less need for distance. I am grateful for this. None of us is so immune to tragedy that we can afford to disdain ways of keeping passion alive in the face of terror.

Notes

[1]   I summarize the film not only for the sake of those readers who have not seen it, but also to circumvent some of the confusion inherent in its alternations between past and present. Like dreams or free associations, *Utz* has a primary-process quality in which present and past exist together, linked by their unconscious meaning. Moreover, in any naturalistic study, such as an analysis or a movie, the details—of dialogue, of background music, of camera angles, in short, all of the nuances of nonverbal communications, either between the characters or between the director and us, the viewers—are profoundly important.

2   Sluizer told the British Film Institute that Nicola Piovani's composition "expresses very profoundly both the tenderness of the Baron von Utz for his porcelain objects as well as his obsession for them" (www.bfi.org.uk/sightandsound/2004_09/filmmusic).

3   In fact, when a colleague tried to send an early version of this paper back to me, her e-mail program Eudora complained that the title would get her computer keyboard washed out with soap.

4   Klein (1927), in "Criminal Tendencies in Normal Children" (pp. 170-185), attributes to Sachs a similar conclusion: "The pervert does not simply permit himself, owing to lack of conscience, what the neurotic represses in consequence of his inhibitions. He found that the conscience of the pervert is not less strict but is simply working in a different way. It permits one part only of the forbidden tendencies to be retained in order to escape from other parts, which seem still more objectionable to the super-ego. What it rejects are desires belonging to the Oedipus complex…." (p. 184). Therefore she was more optimistic than some about a good result in the analysis of people with perversions.

5   It is significant that it is opera singers who draw Utz. Porcelain is as smooth as skin, Utz's grandmother teaches him, and a glorious soprano, as I have indicated elsewhere (Katz, 1997), is soothing, comforting, enlivening, seductive. Like the voice of a mother, it can fill the emptiness within. (As mentioned earlier, Stoller specifically mentions both voice and skin as likely objects of fetishistic attention.) In addition, it may be that music organizes Utz, temporarily quieting the chaos inside him (Winnicott, 1971, pp. 153-154), and as Congreve has famously put it, soothing his savage breast. In his seduction scenarios, Utz experiences himself as an uninhibited actor, in a magnificent and magisterial role. Here again, he establishes a combination of safety and potency that allows him to be passionate.

6   One such movie with a substantial cult following is *The Vanishing*, also directed by Sluizer. This film depicts Raymond, a seemingly ordinary man, a chemistry professor, whose middle-aged life is strictly ordered until passion erupts into it with the puberty of his seductive, engaging fourteen-year-old daughter. He defends

against the sexual and murderous impulses (Katz, 1991) that she arouses by selecting a substitute—a young woman who looks like her—luring her into his car in an obsessively planned scenario, chloroforming her, and then burying her alive. In other words, he resorts to omnipotent control as a defense against overwhelming affect and keeps himself safe by burying his own passions along with their (substitute) "cause." Obviously, Raymond's psychopathology is far more severe than Utz's, and his use of perversion and fetish far more disturbed.

[7]   In rescuing Marta from the horde of rageful men who were pursuing her, he not only saved her virtue (if not her life), but also acquired her.

[8]   In most of the legends of the Prague *Golem*, Rabbi Loew's motives are good; his wish is to create a giant to *protect* the Jews of Prague from the pogroms that threaten them. At first the *golem* does this. But the more he exercises his powers, the less his controller can contain them. The *golem* becomes more violent and more destructive until the people he is protecting come to fear him more than the external enemy. In most versions the Rabbi has to unmake him; in some he escapes and is still living in Prague. The message of the legends is that the power to give life belongs only to God, and that omnipotence is unattainable for humans.

[9]   The aria is a profound commentary on the relationship between Utz and Marta. *Rusalka* is based on Hans-Christian Andersen's well-known story of the little mermaid who saves a mortal man from drowning, falls in love with him, and gives up her glorious voice and the chance for an immortal soul in exchange for a human form in which to woo him. If she wins him, she will survive; if not, she will die. But she can never explain herself to him. In the "Song to the Moon," Rusalka begs the moon to tell the prince of her love. She acquires human form on agreement that she will give up her power of speech, and that if her loved one betrays her, both she and he will be eternally damned. But in the *Rusalka* story, human form is not the same as human flesh. The prince is bewitched by Rusalka's beauty, but he craves a warmth that his sea-born bride cannot give—she is capable of love, but not of sexual passion. And she faces a harder

choice than Andersen's mermaid: She may kill the prince, and so return to her original form and fate. But if she does not, she will become a sea demon, a siren that lures humans to their destruction. Rusalka refuses the killing, wishing her beloved the happiness that will doom her. He belatedly recognizes the depth of their love and follows her, pleading for a kiss of forgiveness. Although her kiss now can bring him only death, he will not be moved. They kiss, and as he dies in her arms, she thanks him for letting her experience love, and commends his soul to God. Then she sinks to the bottom of the water in obedience to her own terrible fate. It is easy to recognize in this story the love between the exquisite water nymph Marta, who can love but cannot tolerate the flames of human passion, and Utz, the prince who needs the flames of a passion that he cannot realize with his own beloved. Neither can survive the other's sexuality, nor can they ever discuss their impasse. Unlike Rusalka and her prince, however, they honor the prohibition until the nearness of Utz's death frees them from their fears of destroying each other.

[10]   For individuals in whom the disappointment in loved ones is very great, the inanimate object is substituted since it can be controlled. Leonardo was notorious for not being able to part with his paintings. Bergmann's (1987) understanding is that Leonardo fell in love with his paintings, not with the sitter, and he suggests that the reason he could not part with the paintings was because his capacity to love a person was blocked. I had a patient who, like Leonardo, for a long time felt safer loving her paintings than a flesh-and-blood beloved, and so could not let go of them. When she did sell one, she created so much chaos in her buyers that they ended up reacting to her with sadism and abandonment—exactly as her former husband had.

[11]   William Wyler's (1965) film *The Collector* is a portrait of another alienated man, an obsessed collector of butterflies. When a huge win at the football pools allows him to buy a manor house with an extensive basement, he expands his impassioned collecting, chloroforms the beautiful woman he's been stalking and imprisons her underground as if she were one of his beautiful dead insects, to be displayed and admired. He loves her, but when she comes close enough to him to stimulate his erotic passions, his face changes

52

visibly, displaying murderous hatred. She dies of a fever because he fears that he would lose her if he exposed the situation to the scrutiny of any doctor who might treat her. After burying her, he begins his search for another woman to collect.

REFERENCES

Bach, S. (1994). The language of perversion and the language of love. Northvale, N.J.: Aronson.

Balzac, H. De (1900). The lilly of the valley. In The works of Honor'e de Balzac (vol. 17, p. 37; E. Marriage, trans.). New York: Society for English and French Literature.

Chasseguet-Smirgel, J. (1978). Reflexions on the connexions between perversion and sadism. *Int. J. Psycho-Anal.*, 59:27-35. Chatwin, B. (1998). Utz. New York: Vintage.

Dimen, M. (2001). Perversion is us. *Psychoanal. Dial.*, 11:325-360.

Etchegoyen, R. H. (1978). Some thoughts on transference perversion. *Int. J. Psycho-Anal.*, 59:45-53.

Freud, S. (1905). Three essays on the theory of sexuality. In J. Strachey, ed. and trans., The complete psychological works of Sigmund Freud, 24 vols. London: Hogarth Press, 1953-1974. 7:125-244.

Freud, S. (1919). A child is being beaten: A contribution to the study of the origin of sexual perversions. Standard Edition, 17:179-204.

Freud, S. (1924). The dissolution of the oedipal complex. Standard Edition, 19:173-179.

Freud, S. (1927). Fetishism. Standard Edition, 21:149-157.

Goldberg, A. (1975). A fresh look at perverse behavior. *Int. J. Psycho-Anal.*, 56:335-342.

Khan, M.M.R. (1979). The role of will and power in perversions. In Alienation in perversion (pp. 197-209). Madison, Conn.: International Universities Press.

Katz, A. (1991). The claustrophobic dilemma. *Round Robin*, 7(3):18-22.

Katz, A. (1997). Faces of abuse: Portrait of a couple. *Psychoanal. Rev.*, 84:753-767.

Klein, M. (1927). Criminal tendencies in children. In Love, guilt and reparation and other works, 1921-1945 (pp. 170-185). Delacorte Press/Seymour Lawrence, 1975.

Klein, M. (1946). Notes on some schizoid mechanisms. In Envy and gratitude and other works, 1946-1963 (pp. 1-24). Delacorte Press/Seymour Lawrence, 1975.

Kohut, H. (1984). How does analysis cure? (A. Goldberg, ed., with the collaboration of P. Stepansky). Chicago: University of Chicago Press.

Marucco, N. C. (1997). The Oedipus complex, castration and the fetish: A revision of the psychoanalytic theory of sexuality. *Int. J. Psycho-Anal.*, 78:351-355.

Muensterberger, W. (1994). Collecting: An unruly passion. New York: Harcourt, Brace.

Nersessian, E. (1998). A cat as fetish: A contribution to the theory of fetishism. *Int. J. Psycho-Anal.*, 79:713-725.

Payne, S. M. (1939). The fetishist and his ego. In R. Fliess, ed., The psychoanalytic reader: An anthology of essential papers with critical introductions (pp. 21-30). New York: International Universities Press, 1962.

Richards, A. K. (2003). A fresh look at perversion. *J. Amer. Psychoanal. Assn.*, 51:1199-1217.

Stoller, R. J. (1985). Presentations of gender. New Haven, Conn.: Yale University Press.

Stein, R. (2003). Why perversion? False love and the perverse pact. *Int. J. Psycho-Anal.*, 86:775-790. Winnicott, D. W. (1971). Contributions in child psychiatry. New York: Basic Books.

Article Citation

Katz, A.W. (2007). Perversion, Fetish, and Creativity. *Psychoanal. Rev.*, 94:943-966, Copyright © 2012, Psychoanalytic Electronic Publishing.

CHAPTER FOUR ભ

American Beauty
Directed by Sam Mendes (1999)

This study of American Beauty was presented in Beijing, China at a scientific meeting in October 2011, sponsored by the Chinese American Psychoanalytic Alliance. It was also presented at several other scientific meetings sponsored by various psychoanalytic institutes, including New York City and London.

Looking at the Film "American Beauty" Through a Psychoanalytic Lens: Parents Revisit Adolescence

In this study of Sam Mendes's Oscar-winning 1999 film, *American Beauty,* I will follow the theme of the developmental journey: the ongoing effort to lay claim to one's life.

Laying claim to a life of one's own is one of the primary tasks of adolescence. However, separation and adulthood are not achieved in one fell swoop, and the search for an authentic satisfying life of one's own can be, and perhaps ideally should be, a life-long endeavor (Levinson, 1978; Anthony, 1993). To do the work of adolescence, a child must create within him or herself psychic space for both childhood and adulthood, and for experimenting with new identities, new beginnings, and new endings (Blos, 1985). The child's parents must do the same, since each new beginning for the child is potentially an end for the parents, and each new ending potentially a beginning.

Between the issues left over from the incomplete work of the parents' own youth, and the adjustments demanded by the awkward, repeated efforts of their child to separate, the parents of adolescent children are under a lot of stress with regard to their own identities— sexual and otherwise—and with beginnings and endings in their own lives (Benedek, 1970).

I strongly believe that parents do not just react when a child's adolescence engulfs a family. They *do* react, of course, but they *act*, too—that is, they also re-engage their own adolescent passions and conflicts. The turmoil of having an adolescent child therefore, is heightened for the parents by their own individual regression.

Regressions of this kind are responsible in no small part, for what has come to be known as the "mid-life crisis." They may result in uncharacteristic behavior in both parents, which in turn disturbs to a greater or lesser degree (depending upon the parents' prior adjustment and psychic flexibility in their relationship with each other, and with their children.) In this chapter, I will show how this phenomenon is illustrated and elaborated in the movie *American Beauty*.

In my study of *American Beauty*, I first focus on the embattled Burnhams: Lester (played by Kevin Spacey), Carolyn (played by Annette Bening), and their teenage daughter, Jane (played byThora Birch). Once upon a time, we are led to believe, the Burnhams got along better than they do at present. "We used to be happy," Lester says. But, something has surely gone wrong, for they are not happy now. In this study, I will examine what I believe to be "what has gone wrong."

Jane is separating from her parents by the usual adolescent means of criticism and withdrawal. In the past, her openness to them had filled some of their pressing emotional needs. Her growing separation, as well as her physical maturation, has shifted both intrapsychic and interpersonal balances in the two parents, and something has broken down (Loewald, 1980). *American Beauty* is the story of this breakdown and what comes of it. I use this film to illustrate my hypothesis about adolescent re-engagements and the work of separation and growth that is always waiting for us, if we can open ourselves to it. (A. Katz, 2002)

Let me try to show what I am talking about by delving beneath the manifest content of this film. Lester and Carolyn were indeed revisiting their own adolescent issues, and not just reacting to their daughter's adolescent issues. Lester laments the fact that Jane no longer talks to him. They used to be pals. He wonders, "What happened to us?" My answer to his question is that his daughter's adolescence stirred up in her parents a parallel revisitation of their own adolescent passions, conflicts, and separations.

The father's unresolved adolescent issues are reawakened now in the context of his daughter and his wife. Carolyn is also revisiting intense adolescent longings and losses, and feels rejected by the uncharacteristic withdrawal of her husband and child. The parents' separate preoccupations with their unfulfilled needs, and the intensity of their wishes to fulfill them, have left Lester and Carolyn withdrawn into private worlds, intolerant of the incursions of others, and unwilling to relinquish their fantasies long enough to be emotionally available to, and supportive of each other. (Benedek, 1970).

Jane is a "typical" sixteen-year-old. It appears that her parents' desire for love and recognition are directed toward her. Although she once was happy to fulfill them, now she can barely tolerate either her mother or her father. She has distanced herself from them, and is confused by feelings that cover the gamut from murderous rage to fear, desire, and love.

In true adolescent style, although she pushes both parents away, she still needs and wants them. Neither parent can deal with her rejection and still be sensitively available to her, nor can either parent support the other to that end. On the contrary, they are disappointed in and defensively detached from each other, while they compete for Jane's now scarce love and support (Colarusso, 1990).

Jane has a best friend, Angela (played by Mena Suvari), who covers up her fear that she is "ordinary" by bragging that she uses sex to get what she wants. Jane's father, Lester, is enchanted with her. Angela loves and encourages this enchantment. She flaunts it aggressively with Jane, who finds it disgusting, but is also jealous. Jane herself bonds with Ricky (played by Wes Bentley), the odd, intense, eighteen-year-old boy next door. Angela calls him a freak, but Jane knows her own mind. She and Ricky make an attachment that facilitates their work of separation from their own parents. Jane's adolescent struggle is interesting, but I want to focus here on what Jane's struggle evokes in her parents, and on the difficult, parallel journeys it catalyzes in them.

In the beginning of the film, Carolyn is very tightly laced and very lonely. Her passions in this now bitter, arid marriage are displaced onto raising perfect American Beauty roses and acquiring power as a realtor. Lester once supported her real-estate work, and still submits to her obsessional need to create a "romantic" atmosphere in the house, even though he finds this "romance" sterile and loveless. He feels shut out and unappreciated, rejected sexually and emotionally by his wife, and deprived of the old pleasures of closeness with his newly taboo daughter. He comments bitterly that the high point of his day is masturbating in the shower. The alienated Lester encounters the teenage Ricky, who is a waiter at a stuffy party. They bond around their mutual defiance of authority. They smoke marijuana and laugh together. When Carolyn fetches him to go home, Lester says, "Okay, Mom."

His adolescent recapitulation hits full stride when he quits the job he hates (engineering a good monetary deal for himself by threatening to expose the fraudulent hypocrisy of his employer/father). He begins to feel powerful and happy. He is galvanized by his crush on seductive Angela. He gets a job as a hash-slinger at a fast food place, drives around singing with joy and aggression, *"American woman, stay away from me! American woman, mama, let me be!"* and buys a red Firebird—all of which evoke for him the seventies, when the teenage Lester still felt the world was open to him. It is hard not to believe that he has regressed to his own adolescent issues, and is reworking his sense of self and identity (Loewald,1979).

Lester wants to feel loved and recognized. He comes alive in his fantasies of a perfect woman. Significantly, he always imagines Angela embedded in crimson rose petals, suggestive of the American Beauty roses to which Carolyn is so passionately attached. Despite the overtly arid and angry relationship with his wife, Lester seems still to desire her. Thus we see Lester reopening his developmental growth, endeavoring to become a strong, independent man (Anthony, 1970). When his wife catches him masturbating in bed, for instance, and attempts to humiliate him, instead of cowering as he used to, he expresses his rage at her refusal to have sex when he then suggests it. He decides to get in shape, lifting weights and jogging.

Carolyn also is revisiting her adolescent issues. As her own sexual and aggressive tensions intensify, she at first reinforces her obsessive-compulsive defenses, creating the "house beautiful" and growing perfect roses. She despises weakness and failure, in herself as much as in others. When she cries out of sadness or disappointment, she cruelly slaps her own face to shut herself up, and tries to program herself to be upbeat. She relies upon superficial "show" to defend against the "messiness" of her strong feelings. She is the more fragile of the two parents.

In the beginning of the film, Carolyn lacks compassion for either herself or her husband. So controlling and judgmental is she that at first the viewer, too, is hard put to feel for her. On repeated viewings of this film, we understand more of the pain covered up by her brittle, rigid exterior. Still, she is not easy to live with. She cannot relinquish control sufficiently to listen to others. Lester, frustrated and infuriated by this, finally gets her attention by throwing a plate of food against the wall of their exquisite dining room. Carolyn knocks on Jane's door looking for comfort, but Jane rejects this bid for alliance and dismisses both of her parents as freaks, which leaves Carolyn feeling alone and furious. Although Jane's developing autonomy is experienced by her parents as abandonment, it also highlights the incompleteness of *their own* adolescent quests for autonomy and fulfillment (Benedek, 1970). Carolyn is not yet able to recognize that her own need to separate is as important as Jane's, so Jane's response, "I'm not in the mood for a Kodak moment," enrages Carolyn. She slaps her daughter's face, as she had earlier slapped her own.

Despite herself and despite her fears, Carolyn's juices are also beginning to rise. She begins an affair with an arch-rival in the real estate business, whose apparent power she covets. His name is Buddy Kane (played by Peter Gallagher), but he calls himself "the King." She rebels against Lester and her daughter, and returns to her own adolescent journey, submitting to a powerful father figure whose strength she hopes to borrow. Her relationship with Buddy reconnects her with both her feminine and masculine strivings. She surrenders to them and to an authentic desire for sexual pleasure and independence. Buddy offers to teach her the secrets of his success. He also initiates her into the thrill of pistol practice, and she gets high on the phallic power that this affords. Like her husband, she too begins to drive around singing defiantly. Her theme song is, "Nobody had better rain on my parade" (Katz, 2002). Carolyn is now able to find joy in passions she was afraid of before. Like Lester, her juices are starting to flow again. She, too, is finding her own inner strength.

Amidst all of this wild activity, Lester and Carolyn are growing— fighting with each other openly now, but approaching each other, too. When she discovers Lester's new car, Carolyn confronts him angrily about not having consulted with her. He stands his ground, compliments her on her new haircut—acquired for Buddy's benefit— approaches her on the couch, and begins to kiss her. Intrigued by his new assertiveness and by his loving gaze, she opens up and enjoys his love and attention. Defensively, she pulls away from him when she notices a beer in his hand, taken over by fear that it might spill on her $4000 couch. In upbraiding 0im, the moment is destroyed. Carolyn still confuses surrender with enforced submission (Ghent, 1990, Katz,1990), and so fears her desires for love and sex with Lester. She returns once again to her obsessional defenses, and he gets angry at her for caring more about the couch than about him. They still do not feel safe with each other—they are too afraid of being taken over—but they are taking more risks.

When Lester discovers Buddy and Carolyn kissing, Buddy—fearful of reprisals—splits the scene forever. Lester tells his wife that he won't be passive and submit to her anymore, essentially relinquishing his old sadomasochistic posture (Katz, 1990). The double blow leaves Carolyn feeling weak, helpless, and frightened. Gun practice gives her a quick high, but she still feels small and tries to shore herself up, saying to herself over and over, "I will not be a victim." She entertains murderous fantasies against Lester. Her new capacities for power and passion fuel her own developmental journey.

While all this is going on, Jane's bond with Ricky next door is deepening. At first she was scared and annoyed by his surreptitious videotaping of her, but after the blow-up with her mother, she poses for him in her window, experimentally baring her breasts. She becomes intrigued with him, reciprocating his voyeurism with assertive, exciting exhibitionism. They surrender to each other and fall in love.

Ricky himself comes from a family that is even more troubled than Jane's. Whereas Jane's family is struggling with the normal stresses that adolescence creates, Ricky has reacted to his adolescent journey by breaking down altogether. We see his mother as a shadowy figure—depressed, and nearly catatonic. His father is a brittle, homophobic, retired marine colonel, a caricature of machismo. He is abusive, violent, abandoning, and invasive—infantilizing his son in a desperate attempt to turn back the clock to the greater comfort he experienced with Ricky as a young child. Neither of Ricky's parents is capable of revisiting adolescence with its demands that they surrender—at least temporarily—to the fantasies within them. Their rigidity and fragility leave them helpless in the face of their son's adolescence which they experience as unrelievedly traumatic (Katz, 2002).

Ricky himself, however, has a distance on his situation that Jane does not yet have on hers. Ricky and his father, Colonel Frank Fitz, once shared a special bond, but this was disrupted when the Colonel (played by Chris Cooper) caught his son, in the first flush of adolescent rebellion, smoking marijuana at fifteen. He cast him out of the house and sent him to military school. Ricky, not a compliant adolescent, got himself expelled from that school. His father beat him, leaving the enraged Ricky to struggle with his own violent impulses. After the beating, Ricky tells Jane, a kid in school picked on him for his haircut, and Ricky snapped. He wanted to kill the kid, and would have, he believes, if they hadn't pulled him off. That's when his dad put him in the mental hospital where they drugged him and kept him for two years. When Jane says, "You must hate him," Ricky, sensing his father's inability to love him in any way other than this perverse, sadomasochistic one, defends him, saying with compassion, "He's not a bad man."

Now out of the hospital, Ricky's obsessional videotaping of the world of objects and people helps him preserve his perspective, and his sanity. He also protects his budding autonomy by living a double life, keeping his controlling, intrusive father in the dark about the things that matter to him. For a while he still appears to be daddy's adored, adoring little boy, but he has continued to smoke marijuana secretly, has developed a very successful business selling it, and has been foiling his father's periodic requests for "wiss" samples by substituting drug-free urine acquired from a client.

Ricky begins to come out in the open when he admits to his father that he has a girlfriend. This dismays Colonel Fitz, who deeply needs his son's love and cannot bear his son's separating from him. His own repressed desires distort his understanding of Ricky, and lead him to dangerous misinterpretations. He catches a glimpse of a transaction between Ricky and Lester; in fact it's a marijuana deal, but Colonel Fitz concludes that they have a sexual connection. He projects his own repudiated fantasies onto Lester and Ricky. When Ricky comes home, he beats him brutally, saying, "I'd rather you were dead than be a faggot." Ricky's work of separation, however eccentric, is well under way, and he maintains his sense of himself even under this attack. He refuses to hit his father back even when his father, seeking any kind of reconnection with his son, begs him to. He refuses to submit to his father's view of life and is able to realize, not without compassion, what "a sad little man" the Colonel is.

After the fight, Ricky asks Jane to leave home with him. She agrees, and tells Angela about her intention. Angela once again attacks Jane and Ricky as freaks, but Ricky defends Jane and challenges Angela's pretensions, exposing the fears and jealousies that she tries so hard to conceal.

We see a poignant scene between Lester and the now bereft Angela, in which Lester declares his yearning for her. "You're the most beautiful thing I've ever seen," he says, and begins to undress her. She encourages him in an attempt to reassure herself of her own desirability, but he comes to his adult senses when he realizes that she is a frightened girl underneath her sexual bravado. In a beautiful, transforming moment, he refuses to let Angela submit to him. He covers her with a blanket, reassures her that she is beautiful, that everything is okay, and that any man would consider himself very, very lucky to be with her. He then takes her into the kitchen and feeds her, a metaphor that represents his turning away from his obsessive need to be eighteen again and crossing over to a nurturant guiding stance toward the next generation—a phase termed by Erikson (1950) as "generativity vs. stagnation" (p231). Thus Lester helps Angela return to her own precociously rejected adolescence, at peace with herself, and no longer hiding behind her pretensions (Anthony, 1970).

Lester has returned to the parental stance, having, I believe, gone through a tremendous adolescent regression and reworking. Angela also has visibly returned to a less defended, more authentic self. Lester asks her about his own daughter, admitting how hard it is for them to talk to each other these days. Angela tells him that Jane is in love. He says with appreciative pleasure, "Good for her" (Erikson, 1950). His recent re-engagement with his own issues of love, power, and autonomy has made it possible for him to empathize in a new way with his daughter. Wistfully he recalls how happy he was with his wife when Jane was younger. He looks at a photo of Carolyn, Jane and himself, and smiling says, "I feel great!" (Colarusso, 1990).

In the beginning of this movie, we see Lester begin his journey as the father of Jane's adolescence, and his control over his sexual and aggressive impulses are shaky. His defenses have become destabilized in the face of his own reawakened adolescent passions (Loewald, 1979). In connecting with his fantasies of power and sex, of overthrowing and outsmarting the authorities, and in breaking out of the bondage he experienced at work and in his marriage, I believe he became able to negotiate his own conflicted desires in a healthier manner. He could then give up fantasies of perfect, idealized self and other, feel good about himself, however flawed, and be

63

genuinely happy when his daughter finds love with the boy next door. His new compassion and strength also allow a renewed appreciation and love for his wife.

Meanwhile, Lester's new vitality has attracted not only Angela, but also Ricky's father, whose brittle homophobic controls have collapsed during the adolescent revisitation brought on by his own child's physical and psychological maturation. Reawakened passions can have a dark side and, in *American Beauty*, that side is played out in Colonel Fitz. This harsh, repressed man, whose mantra is "structure and discipline," uses rigid controls to defend against unmetabolized homosexual yearnings. He is in turmoil over his son's adolescence, and the passions and conflicts it has revived within him. Ricky was once a small child whom he could control and love without danger. His love for the now sexually mature Ricky terrifies him, and his rigid defenses against it have become destabilized (Benedek, 1970). He alternates between treating Ricky as the child he no longer is, and occasional violent beatings. These last-ditch defenses break down. Colonel Fitz hates what he cannot bear to acknowledge in himself. Stirred by Ricky's physical maturation and his own adolescent urges rising up—(Katz, 2002) he displaces the homosexual desire that overtakes him onto Ricky's supposed partner, Lester, who then becomes the object of his desire.

So, right before Lester's encounter with Angela, Colonel Fitz approaches Lester in the garage where he is working out. Colonel Fitz is shaking, soaking wet from the rain; he can barely talk. The downpour in the movie beautifully represents the torrent of feeling drenching him. his own outpouring of messy feelings. Misinterpreting Lester's concern for him, he kisses Lester in a sudden breakdown of his fragmenting defenses. Lester gently tells him that he has the wrong idea. His new security and psychic strength as a person and as a man are marked by the calm, gentle way he responds to this frantic advance. Lester's compassion and lack of anger do not spare the terribly vulnerable Colonel Fitz a humiliation so deep that he eventually must silence the witness to it. In an attempt to reinstate his manhood, he stalks Lester—who himself is in a contented reverie of newfound peace. Colonel Fitz shoots Lester and kills him.

This somber denouement makes clear that: there are no more guarantees in a second adolescence than in a first one; parental revisitations of early struggles with desire and separation do not necessarily eventuate in growth; severe repression is potentially far more dangerous than a rich fantasy life, however wild and chaotic it may occasionally be. In this movie, it is not the people with the rageful and sexual fantasies, but only the person who cannot bear to know what's inside of him. It is he who solves his problems by killing the object of his desire.

For Carolyn and Lester, revisitation of their adolescent journeys brings pain and disappointment, but also joy. For the Fitz parents, there is only pain and decompensation.

I keep wondering why the director foretells Lester's death as the film opens; death is present from the very beginning. Although we see lives being transformed throughout, we know that one life will be over by the time the movie ends. Why does Lester have to die just after struggling so hard to achieve a new inner and outer balance, and having indeed achieved a new, vital sense of self and other? Why is this flowering so tragically and violently cut off just as it is beginning to be enjoyed? It seems so senseless. Perhaps this is the director's point: we all die. How we come to death is beyond our control. Development is risky. All we can do is make the journey in the most meaningful way we can. This journey may be a search for inner truth, but to find truth doesn't guarantee life—only the capacity to live fully and authentically. There are no guarantees as to how others will receive what we give or do not give. Perhaps this says something powerful and humbling to us as analysts as well.

In this movie there is a passionate scene of bonding between Ricky and Jane when he shows her a video in which a discarded bag—a piece of trash—dances in a buffeting wind. This is a dance of life to Ricky, breathtakingly beautiful and moving. Something ugly is lovingly accepted, and in the acceptance is transformed. The bag, too, displays the beauty of acceptance in its surrender to the wind. This movie is about surrendering to the wind, a metaphor for the life force and the life course. Laying claim to a life of one's own in the ongoing journey of life involves surrender—not enforced or unthinking submission—but willing surrender—to knowledge—knowledge of the fantasies, feelings and conflicts within the self, and knowledge of what is out there. Rilke (1986) poetically captures this concept, *"He who pours himself out like a stream is acknowledged at last by Knowledge: and she leads him enchanted through the harmonious country that finishes often with starting, and with ending begins"...* (Rilke, Sonnets to Orpheus, second part,12)

So the forces of growth and the forces of death interact in *American Beauty* in complex ways, as they do in life, and perhaps particularly in adolescence. While Lester is enduring the final, decisive confrontations of his own life, Carolyn is becoming a woman who can enjoy her own phallic power and aggression, test out in fantasy its violent potential, and still rediscover her love for the husband at whom she feels such rage. Tragically, her achievement comes too late for a happy ending with Lester, now dead at the hands of a man who could neither entertain nor contain his own fantasies.

The difference between fantasy and action is poignantly portrayed at the end of this movie. Carolyn comes home with the fantasy of killing her husband, repeating with rage, "I will not be a victim." Then she throws her gun in the hamper, hugs his clothes hanging in the closet, and crumples to the floor weeping—very different from her crying before—allowing herself to mourn the idea of his death, as previously she could not. It is not clear whether she has already seen that he is dead. Her fantasy of gaining power by killing him has been shaken. She has become sufficiently strong in herself to face the reality of what she would lose if he were actually to die. She recognizes that the person she wanted dead was also the person she loved. This integration of the loved and hated husband, the result of her struggles, marks a transformation in her that will endure, in spite of the tragic reality of Lester's death (Klein, 1975).

Conclusion

Parenthood affords adults many opportunities to regress to, and potentially rework, past and present intrapsychic issues in parallel with their children. So does analysis, as patients regress and reexperience buried feelings (that are stirred up in their analysts, as well).

What's so hard, as well as rewarding about what we do as psychoanalysts, is the stirring up of these feelings, and the longings and conflicts that go with them. Not just in them, but in ourselves as well. Although challenging, this provides opportunities to revisit our own deeper issues. It is in this way that we become more open to our patients, more able to hear and interpret. Both they and we grow in the process. If we cannot tolerate our own revisitings, we may fail our patients by foreclosing, or acting out, their deepest wishes and fears.

REFERENCES

Anthony, E.J. (1970). "The Reactions of Parents to Adolescents and to Their Behavior in Parenthood, Its Psychology and Psychopathology", eds. E. James Anthony and Therese Benedek. Boston: Little Brown and Co.

Anthony, E.J. (1993). Psychoanalysis and environment. In "The Course of Life", Vol. 6: Late Adulthood. Eds. George H. Pollock and Stanley I. Greenspan. Madison, Conn.: International Universities Press.

Benedek, T. (1970). Parenthood During the Life Cycle, in "Parenthood Its Psychology and Psychopathology", eds. E. James Anthony and Therese Benedek. Boston: Little Brown and Co, 185-206.

Blos, P. (1985). Toward an Altered View of the Male Oedipus Complex: The Role of Adolescence, in Blos, "Son and Father: Before and Beyond the Oedipus Complex", N.Y.: The Free Press, 135-173.

Colarusso, C. (1990). The Effect of Biological Parenthood on Separation-Individuation Processes in Adulthood. "Psychoanalytic Study of the Child" 45. New Haven:Yale University Press.

Erikson, E.H. (1950) "Childhood and Society". New York:W.W. Norton & Company.

Ghent, E. (1990. Masochism, Submission and Surrender: Masochism as a Perversion of Surrender. Contemporary Psychoanalysis, 26, 108-136.

Katz, A. (1990). Paradoxes of Masochism, Psychoanalytic Psychology 7:225-242.

Katz, A. (2002). Fathers Facing Their Daughters' Emerging Sexuality: The Return of the Oedipal. Psychoanalytic Study of the Child. 57:270-293.

Klein, M. (1975) Love, Guilt and Reparation & Other Works, 1921-1945. Delacorte Press/Seymour Lawrence.

Levinson, D.J. (1978) "The Seasons of a Man's Life". New York: Ballantine Books. pp.221-256.

Loewald, H.W. (1979). The Waning of the Oedipus Complex". JAPA: 27:751-776.

Loewald, H.W(1980). Comments on Some Instinctual Manifestations of Superego Formation. "Papers on Psychoanalysis". New Haven: Yale University Press, pp. 326-341.

Rilke, Rainer Maria: "The Sonnets to Orpheus: (Touchstone: 1986) quoted in: Zornberg, Avivah Gottlieb (1995). Genesis: The Beginning of Desire. (5755/1995). The Jewish Publication Society. Philadelphia & Jerusalem.

CHAPTER FIVE ∞

The Vanishing
Directed by George Sluizer (1988)

Destiny Revised: The Illusion of Free Choice
A Study of Claustrophobia in "The Vanishing"
Derived from the Dutch film, Directed by George Sluizer

PROLOGUE
The Quest for Knowledge from Within the Self and from Another

The quest for knowledge and truth can either result in a creative, inspiring experience, that offers a sense of power and self-direction, or it can lead to a trap, in which one person may feel criticized, controlled, humiliated, squashed or destroyed. In the psychoanalytic situation, two people, psychoanalyst and analysand, work and play creatively together to uncover or discover intrapsychic, interpersonal and historical truths. For the analysand, it may feel wonderful to be understood, and a relief to be known, darker side and all, and still be appreciated.

In the film *The Vanishing*, two of the characters, Rex (portrayed by Gene Bervoets) and Raymond (played by Bernard-Pierre Donnadieu), become obsessed with intellectual control and knowing. Raymond prizes intellectual knowledge and control. He is the detached head of his somber family, which consists of his wife and two adolescent daughters. As a teacher, he tyrannically controls his student's test time. He insists that he's right about the age of a stranger in the roadside store even after the man corrects him. He is extremely controlled and controlling.

Rex and Saskia (played by Johanna ter Steege) are a Dutch couple traveling through France on vacation. At a rest stop Saskia goes into a store to buy soda and mysteriously disappears. Rex becomes obsessed with learning the details of what actually happened to Saskia. He dismisses his own intuitive sense that she is dead. Suddenly Raymond appears and introduces himself to Rex. Rex yields himself up to Raymond, the man he likens to lightening, and who his instincts and reason tell him is responsible for Saskia's disappearance. Rex's grief at losing Saskia, and his murderous rage at Raymond, are then denied. He replaces his dread with awe and childish hope that he will finally get his Saskia back. He cannot accept his own darker side, and the guilt he feels for leaving Saskia alone in the dark tunnel to look for gas. He ignores her panic screaming, "Rex! Rex!" and continues to leave her alone in the tunnel.

Claustrophobia and Raymond Lemorne

In this paper, I will focus on claustrophobia as portrayed in the character, Raymond. The film opens and closes with an image of a praying mantis, an animal in which the female is known to devour the male after copulation. This marks the theme of danger due to sexual union between man and woman. Sexuality is here portrayed as more than castrating; it is literally annihilating. The present as a new edition of the past reverberates in this film. For example, Raymond gazed at Rex from the same balcony that Raymond, the child, watched the people in the square before he took a dramatic leap. I propose that Raymond's character structure is related to a past and present sense of physical and psychic mortal danger associated both with attachment and with sexual and aggressive impulses and desires.

When we first see Raymond, he is filmed through the closed window of his car, the light making a diagonal line separating his head from his body—an image that defines his state of being. His intellect and thoughts are not integrated with his emotions and body. Who is Raymond Lemorne—a name that means dull or dead—and how did he get to be this way? He calls himself a sociopath, yet we see a detached, compulsive man with hysterical features, including severe claustrophobia. He lives a responsible, middle

class life with his family. I hope to throw some light on the dark mystery of Raymond Lemorne.

Raymond, a man in his forties, lives an ordinary life with his wife and two adolescent daughters. Both the wife and older daughter seem subdued, sullen and somewhat depressed; the younger daughter is lively and seductive with her father. On an outing with his family, he hears his daughters scream that a child is drowning, and he leaps without thinking from a very high bridge to save the drowning girl. This is his second dangerous leap. The film's presentation of Raymond's childhood memory of his first leap is jarring. Although Raymond says he is sixteen years old, he looks much younger (six years old). We see him confined on a tiny balcony, looking at, but not part of, the bustle below in the town square. He looks clean, proper and overprotected. He is reading a picture book.

The nature of the picture in the book was not clear, inviting me to call forth my own fantasy of what he was reading. My fantasy might be useful in illuminating latent conflict in Raymond, just as the analyst's fantasies during a session may help to illuminate what is going on with the analysand. It was only after repeated viewings of this movie, and much reflecting on its meanings, did my fantasy emerge that the picture in Raymond's book was an illustration from the fairy tale, *"Jack and the Beanstalk."* I then mused about the content and meaning of this story and how it might be related to Raymond's struggle. In this story, Jack's mother sent him into the world to sell/separate from the cow/milk producing mother to get money to take care of them. When he traded the cow for 3 beans, she demeaned him for being a foolish, inept little boy, rather than a capable young man. She neither understood nor validated him for the potential value of the seeds/sperm he brought her. In disgust, she threw the beans on the ground, and a giant beanstalk/phallus grew on that spot. By climbing up the beanstalk, he entered a space in which he found a goose who laid golden eggs, but he could only possess this goose if he first killed the giant who ruled this space. The giant's wife protected him by hiding him in her oven (womb).

Could we think of this space above the earth as a place of fantasy, a place to play out competitive, murderous urges as well as loving ones? In the classic fairytale, Jack heroically slew the giant and brought the magical goose home to his mother, thereby rescuing her from poverty and unhappiness. It is interesting that my fantasy was of a boy who was struggling both with pre-oedipal and oedipal conflicts, and who relied heavily on magical power, and grandiosity to change his destiny. In the

71

fairy tale, he corrected his mother's opinion of him as inadequate, unmanly and impotent by venturing on a dangerous journey and slaying the giant (his rival) so that he could retrieve the goose that laid the golden eggs to enrich his mother and gain her love, respect and admiration. As Bettelheim (1976) points out, Jack initially uses magic to achieve power and love, but at the end of the story he cuts down the magical beanstalk, indicating that he could now separate from magical ways of achieving power and begin to move on to more realistic ways of being competent and valued. This no doubt is related to his coming of age and separating from mother.

Based on my fantasy, I postulate that Raymond, as a child, felt disillusioned in his efforts to please his mother, and be admired by her as powerful and manly. I hypothesize that Raymond was at risk of being engulfed by his mother, or demeaned and quashed by her, and that his struggles for self-esteem, self-direction, and self-control seemed useless. During his development he wanted to disentangle himself from his need for her, and her impact and power over him. He also desperately wanted to free himself from his overwhelming surge of wild impulses including sexual desire and murderous rage. As Loewald (1980) points out, a strong father was needed to both protect him and mother from an incestuous union, as well as to serve as a positive male model with whom competition is safe, and identification possible. I hypothesize that like Jack, Raymond did not have this kind of father, but unlike Jack he has never cut down the magical "giant beanstalk."

At age sixteen, Raymond jumps from a balcony. This was a grandiose, magical, yet suicidal jump to escape his entrapment, and to kill mother off in him, to at last be free and separate. He survives but is permanently injured with the loss of two fingers, as well as a broken arm. At age 42, he tells Rex that he was in control of what he was doing, and that he decided to do what others only think about doing. He explains he did this in order to change his destiny, to change what was "predetermined." He took charge of his own castration, thereby gaining grandiose, magical power over his father. I interpret this as Raymond punishing himself for wanting to sexually unite with his mother. Exquisite, absolute control of his destiny, and nothing less was his goal. This is the kind of control we might associate with a troubled latency aged child, whose emotions have not been properly validated and organized by his parents. Raymond is oriented toward excessive control and foreclosure of unruly emotions.

The early memory of the jump both reveals and screens. It represents the actual events, desires, fears, and thoughts at the different time periods of his life. This quest for omnipotent control led to poor reality testing, poor impulse control, and a masochistic solution.

As a grown man, Raymond took a second dangerous leap to save a young drowning girl, in the presence of his two adolescent daughters, Simone and Denise (played by Bernadette Le Sache and Tania Latarjet). They decree him a hero. But then, he cannot tolerate his daughter's idealizing him. I believe that he feels paradoxically both trapped by their pleasure in him, and wildly excited by it. Moreover, their labeling him a hero may be a role that feels like a trap. He then is compelled to escape from it by proving that he is the opposite. He thereby hopes to establish his freedom and separate identity. He criticizes his daughters to ward them off. He tells them they are being excessive and is compelled then to devise an action that is the most horrible thing he can think of—sadistic act whereby he hopes to magically control the dangers from within and without. The sado-masochistic behavior offers grandiose protection insofar as it is a pattern of capturing the present and future rather than being caught unawares. The dangers of failure, disappointment, and rejection for Raymond is probably devastating and even annihilating. Since it is impossible to be unerringly, unendingly pleasing, good and heroic, equilibrium is regained through sadistic or masochistic control (Katz, 1990).

Also, to be rejected for one's evil deeds is far less painful and disorganizing than to be rejected for one's longings, needs for attachment and for oneself. Raymond believes that if he is really a good person, he should be incapable of doing anything bad. He does not understand ambiguity and illusion; he does not know how to create or enjoy a potential space in which he is idealized by his daughters, while still feeling separate and in control of his impulses and wishes. He is overwhelmed by his daughters' love and excitement. So, to remain intact and unchanged in his ordinary life with his family, and to defend against being overtaken by his daughters' love and excitement, he plans an action which simultaneously would stifle the wild excitement in him and in his daughters.'

That it was his pubescent, seductive daughter, Denise, who was his nemesis, is underlined in one scene in the movie. In this scene, he repeatedly rehearses the crime he is planning. He picks Denise up at school, feeds her pastry, tweaks her nose playfully and seductively. When Denise is puzzled by him locking the car door, he explains that he is protecting her from falling out of the car to her death while they drive. And indeed he was protecting her from his own libidinal and murderous impulses. His intended victim (Saskia) was a substitute for his flirtatious daughter, Denise. She is the real present dangerous (incestuous) exciting love object in his life. Not surprisingly, his ultimate replacement for Denise was Saskia, an eerie look-alike for Denise. It seems to me that his daughter Denise also represented himself as an adolescent with his own terrifying impulses and desires for attachment and sexual pleasure with mother.

In order to gain control of his overwhelming impulses towards his daughters, and to avoid annihilation anxiety, Raymond plans an action that involves seducing a woman into his car, chloroforming her and burying her alive. He repeatedly rehearses the details of the seduction and crime. At times he is controlled, scientific and precise, at other times romantic, playful and lyrical, as though his aim was to seduce for love, not for entrapment and destruction. The background music is lilting, as is his manner, as he sings ta, da, dum. The scene is shot from above, so that he appears to be small, evoking a sense of his vulnerability and childish self. He is learning the French language—simple sentences, which are reminiscent of childhood—of the toddler.

The acquisition of language is an awesome achievement in a child's development, and often coincides with toilet training and the separation-individuation phase of development. In this film there are repeated themes of learning language and playing with language—beginning with the word games between Saskia and Rex. He is teaching her French, and she then tries to communicate with Raymond in a childish French, Raymond teaches himself to speak English and German in order to seduce his victim, and finally Rex and Raymond playing with names and what happens to names

when people get connected, get married (i.e. what happens to individual identities).

The word that Raymond struggles with is "hitch"—"Would you please help me hitch my trailer to my car," and finally changes it to "attach." The double meaning of hitch—attaching two things or getting hitched and married—suggest that he has a great deal of difficulty in nurturing or libidinal attachment to another, and that the earliest maternal love relationship was intensely disappointing. Only when frustrations and disappointments are of moderate intensity does the small child learn to deal with them in a constructive, growth enhancing way. The rapprochement child (14-24 months) experiences disappointments and disillusionments reminding him that he is separate from, and not one with mother. When these disappointments are of moderate intensity, he can then move to the next step of separateness and connectedness. In normal development, the child gradually gives up the magical illusion of omnipotence and symbiotic oneness characteristic of the practicing child and increasingly experiences himself as a separate person. If during his youth he feels his ideas and feelings are not valued and appreciated, then he loses a sense that he has some part in his own destiny. His biography is felt to be totally written by mother (and also father), in other words, it is predestined. This is, I conjecture, a possible scenario of Raymond's history, and why he was compelled to take a dramatic action (a leap) at age 16 to "change what is predestined."

When Raymond tells Rex, "You didn't know her [Saskia] long enough to not love her." Raymond clues us into his own rage and bitter disappointment in early love objects. As he told his wife in a detached manner, "I may be the only man left in France who has known only one woman," presumably meant to reassure her that he is not having an extramarital affair but letting us know that he no longer has any illusions or hope of finding love or pleasure with a woman, except in his psychotic state while practicing his crime.

It is significant that it is only while practicing his seduction of a woman that Raymond seems self-assured, walking and moving in a graceful, animated manner. When he approaches a real woman, he seems awkward and wooden, and unable to deal with spontaneous dialogue that had not been in his prepared script (a script which seemed to assume that the unknown woman would of course trust him when he invited her into his car). When a woman invites him to have coffee with her, obviously interested in him, he becomes flustered, and turns his head away from her in an embarrassed gesture. He takes his pulse, and it is racing; his goal is to remain unaffected by women. Total control of his own excitements, as measured by his pulse, is what he is determined to have.

Paradoxically, with many of the women who he approaches, he is consistently inept, and unmanly. But with Saskia he comes alive. He watches and listens to Saskia intently as she shares with him her excitement about driving on the highway and her attraction to his key chain with the letter "R" (the libidinal gift from his lively daughter, Denise). Saskia is an exciting woman, and he becomes strong and manly in her presence, and because of this he is at great risk of being swept away. Because this is the very thing that terrifies him, *i.e.* her power to excite him, he is driven to ensnare her into his car and deaden her.

Transitional Objects

There were several scenes in the film which were puzzling. I came to believe that they hold important clues into Raymond's psychology. Their meaning slowly unfolds through my own free associations. For example, on first viewing, I was puzzled as to why Raymond would not rescue the little girl's doll from the river. It seems to me that the doll is a transitional object, which according to Winnicott (1975) facilitates the development of self as separate from others while still preserving a connection to another. Raymond saved the child physically, but not psychically, the child within himself is smothered, drowning, foreclosed, not connected or integrated into his present self. He is wooden, overtrained, overpolite. There is no transitional space to play. Raymond is deadly serious: good and evil, life and death are the stakes.

Raymond's Inner Representation of Father Enactments and Reconstructions

Raymond's relationship to his father as a child is never explicitly revealed. One scene that clues us into Raymond's relationship to his father involves Rex viciously hitting and kicking Raymond. This occurs when Rex reconnects with Raymond several years after Saskia disappears. My first thought about this was that Rex impotently attacked Raymond. I was empathizing with Rex, and really wanted him to kill Raymond, paralleling Rex's wish and fear that Raymond die. Unfortunately, the fear was greater than the wish. He could have killed him at that moment. His first words to Raymond are puzzling. They are, "I was afraid you were dead."

This scene disturbed me. I wished he were dead. I came to realize that I was resistant to empathizing with Raymond. When I overcame this resistance, it became clear to me that it was Raymond who was rendered impotent, helpless, a cowering little boy who had no way to empower himself and retaliate or defend himself when viciously abused by Rex, a representation of his father. This scene now suggests to me representations of Raymond's father as punitive and terrorizing of the young Raymond. According to Loewald (1980), a strong, yet kind father would have both provided a protection against engulfment by the mother, as well as a defense against acting out incestuous pleasures with the mother. This would have enabled him to be aggressive and competitive with father, while still safe to have father's and mother's love and protection.

My earlier fantasies of Jack and the Beanstalk corroborate my impressions from this film's sequences of a dangerous, destructive father and a needy, overprotective, and demeaning mother. Since Raymond is a character in a movie, and not a patient who can play with this material and give us feedback, we cannot either prove or disprove any of these hypotheses. Still, I hope that there is value in what I have written here insofar as it does demonstrate ways of being, working and playing, that is part of real life, both in and out of the clinical setting. As Harry Stack Sullivan said, "All of us are much more human than otherwise."

Raymond's Claustrophobic Dilemma

Toward the end of the film, we learn that Raymond is severely claustrophobic, and suddenly we understand that this film with its rich and varied symbols and images affords us a powerful illumination into some of the conflicts, defenses and interpersonal consequences of claustrophobia.

The claustrophobia of Raymond represents his defensive attempt to create a sense of space and freedom of movement so that he will not be vulnerable to entrapment and engulfment by the object of his desires/fears object. He enjoys women and later enjoys Rex whose name means king, but only from a distance. He is intent on looking, gazing and taking in with his eyes and with photographs (he is an avid photographer). He captures and devours the object of desire from a distance with his eyes, or with photographs.

The claustrophobic symptom did not work, because he was feeling overwhelmed by the stimulation of his adolescent daughter. When his sexual impulses threatened to break through, I believe that Raymond became overwhelmed with "annihilation anxiety." He could not use fantasy or feelings to know and to resolve his traumatic state. Were Raymond a real person, he would remind me of McDougal's "normopath," since he is to all appearances a stable, highly functioning professional man. His split off primitive conflicts, terrors and desires, are expressed through somatic symptoms, or through action, not through symbolic use of language and fantasy (McDougal,1989).

Raymond's ultimate defense involves obsessive preoccupation with devising and executing an act that involves doing something with a physical body—in the first case, a leap with his own body, and in the second instance, entrapping the body of another. Freud (1901) observed that the chronic symptoms of claustrophobia, agoraphobia and fear of heights, all are anxieties relating to the function of the body.

Instead of a conversion symptom to contain traumatic anxiety, Raymond, in a trancelike psychotic state, devised a dramatic action, which would serve to protect his normal functioning self and his significant objects. In this action he would bury another's body, which would be for him burying both his own passions and those of his exciting daughter. Terrified of being

78

engulfed by a woman, Raymond searches for mastery, selfhood and separateness. Ferenzi (1921, p.357) states "The psychoanalysis of numerous dreams of neurotic claustrophobia explains the fear of being buried alive as the transformation into dread of the wish to return to the womb. Moreover, from this narcissistic point of view, every sexual act, every sacrifice to a woman is a loss, a kind of castration, to which the offended ego may react with fear of death." To the fear of castration, I would add the fear of loss of a separate self.

It would appear that Raymond's passions, involving heterosexual and homosexual desires, as well as murderous rage, previously buried and contained by his obsessive-compulsive defenses and by his claustrophobia, had erupted during three periods of his life—at age 6, and age 16—and age 42, when his younger daughter was seductive with him. His passions are fired by the object of desire (his adolescent seductive daughter), and his solution to overwhelming anxiety became to bury the object of desire—or a substitute. The idea of burying alive probably connotes some primitive belief that the object will be thereby preserved—contained, but not really destroyed.

The sadism of Raymond is defensive and also gratifying to him. Raymond, generally joyless, comes alive at the moment he impulsively leaps from the balcony at the age of 16, when he is rehearsing his plan for the kidnapping, and again when he is alone in the car with Rex in the process of executing his next defiance of destiny. He is attracted to Rex, and mistakes Rex's obsessive perseverance for strength, and misunderstands Rex's interest in him as love and attention. I believe Rex becomes for him the strong, kind father. Rex says, I will not hurt you. I just want to know (what happened to Saskia). But Raymond cannot trust Rex to forgive him for his cruelty; just as when a child, he may have believed that his aggressive and loving fantasies caused his father to be harshly punitive and restrictive. He experienced father, if the two screen memories are illuminating, as someone who cruelly restricts and punishes, and not someone who can survive healthy competition while still respecting his son's quest for love and power. Normal competition with men, as in the Tour de France, was certainly not in Raymond's present repertoire. Nor is there evidence that through identification with a beloved father did Raymond develop a healthy superego—a healthy way of both controlling murderous and incestuous impulses while having ongoing sexual and relational pleasures.

Raymond's crime was a kind of enactment, I believe, in which he got Saskia, and then Rex, to experience the desires and terrors of his own childhood, still buried within him in some dark, inaccessible corner of his psyche. The longing for sexual pleasure and loving connectedness was wed to the terrors of being trapped physically, and smothered psychically, resulting in, metaphorically being buried alive. I believe that the screams of Saskia and Rex represented or replaced his own unheard, unvoiced inner screams.

For Raymond love and excitement are dangerous since they are associated with bondage, abuse and psychic death. Raymond's adjustment is a brittle, schizoid, perfectionistic stance: detached and kind with his family, detached and cruelly demanding with his students. When his younger daughter reawakens his passions, and he coincidentally obeys his daughters' pleas that he heroically jump from a bridge to save a drowning little girl, he is in peril of regression to the masochistic bondage of his youth. To escape this peril, he entraps a mother/daughter substitute so that he can remain free and save his daughter's life.

The Vanishing offers a remarkable view into the relatively unexplored human problem of claustrophobia. The wished for and feared container—womb, represented throughout the movie in the relationships and situations that the characters experience—offers joy, protection and power, on the one hand, and entrapment, castration and loss of self, on the other.

A poem by Emily Dickenson comes to mind. She deals with the issue of the conditions for learning truth:

Tell all the Truth but tell it slant –
Success in Circuit lies
Too bright for our infirm Delight
The Truth's superb surprise
As Lightning to the children eased
With explanation kind
The Truth must dazzle gradually –
Or every man be blind.

The truth, which Oedipus insisted on knowing, blinded him; the truth, once known by Rex, takes his breath and life away.

REFERENCES

Benjamin, J. *(1988). The Bonds of Love*. New York: Pantheon Books.

Bettelheim, B. (1976). *The Uses of Enchantment.* New York: Alfred A. Knopf.

Freud, S. (1901). Standard Edition VI:182.

Loewhald, H. (1980) Papers on psychoanalysis, "The Waning of the Oedipus Complex" Yale University Press, New York and London.

Ferenczi, S. Bridge symbolism and the Don Juan Legend, 1921. In "Further contributions to the Theory and Technique of Psychoanalysis," (V2), Bruner Mazel, 1980, New York.

Katz, A. W. (1990). Paradoxes of Masochism, *Psychoanalytic Psychology,* McDougal, J. (1989). *Theaters of the Body.* New York: W.W. Norton & Co.

Winnicott, D.W. (1975) Through Pediatrics to Psychoanalysis, "Hate in the Countertransference" (1947) and "Transitional Objects and Transitional Phenomena" (1951). New York, Basic Books, Inc.

CHAPTER SIX ↷

Proof
Directed by Jocelyn Moorhouse (1991)

Memory Revised—Psychic Reality and Psychic Change: A
Therapeutic Journey

In this study of the Australian film *"Proof"* a blind photographer named Martin (played by Hugo Weaving) is searching for proof that his mother lied to him. He is compelled to hold onto this belief, which shapes his current reality. Yet, he also is searching for proof that his mother did not lie to him. Only then can he relinquish his bitter representation of his mother and begin to trust others.

In this film the paradox of a blind photographer prods us to reexamine concepts of seeing and knowing vis-a-vis inner and outer space, and to study the interplay between psychic and external reality, as well as the interplay between internal and external objects. Questions related to early loss, memory, reconstruction, and mutative factors are discussed.

This film presents us with a portrait of an adult man who is congenitally blind. On an unconscious level, his blindness signifies castration at conception–at the moment of his mother and father's fantasied passionate sexual union. He feels punished due to a whim of fate–here doled out by mother and father in their sexual union–before he even has a self, and before he has his own desires.

Through microanalysis of transference between characters, and of my empathic and countertransference reactions, I examine the effects of traumatic loss in this man's life when a young boy, and the defenses he uses. His interpretation and beliefs drive his perceptions and behavior in his adulthood. His blindness is a reality and a metaphor for not knowing. His use of a camera and photographs represent his wish to know—for pleasure, safety, reality testing, protection and growth—depending upon the circumstances and person he uses them with.

The nature of memory, including screen memories, and defenses against knowing the truth are explored. The same inanimate object (camera and photos) may serve to hold on to a defensive, rigid, sadomasochistic orientation in life when used with one person, or paradoxically serve to open up doors to new experiences, perceptions, new beliefs about old memories, and a more flexible orientation in the world when used with another person. The implication of this for the analytic situation will be drawn.

Introduction

The Australian film "Proof" (1992) directed by Jocelyn Moorhouse is a study of psychic reality in a 32-year-old blind man. The film shows how Martin's psychic reality developed in a particular way, and how it changed (that is, how he changed). Psychic reality includes unconscious beliefs, perceptions, and behavior. They are parallel processes, determining both the choice of love object and the way of relating to that object, repeating the internal drama in external relationships. The struggle for growth and development may lead the protagonist to find a person who helps him resume his blocked development. I use my experience with the film *"Proof"* in much the same way that I use my experience with an analysand. The film affords an avenue to understand the subject's emotions and intra-psychic conflicts, and how they play out in his seeking safety, pleasure, and power in interpersonal relationships. The keys to sorting out psychic reality from historical reality are the distortions and enactments in the analytic situation between patient and analyst (or in the film between characters).

This film also provides clues as to what is healing or curative, what is therapeutic in the characters' words and experiences with one another, and what is pathological. Needless to say, transference and countertransference provide the route to understanding in the clinical situation. Likewise, in the film transference between characters, and shared experiences by characters, and countertransference in the viewer, provide the route to understanding and learning about psychic structure and psychic change from the film.

Just as analysands teach and surprise me about what I thought I understood, so, too, the film *"Proof"* taught me new ways of understanding fetish and transitional objects, extending Greenacre's (1969) views on these two phenomena. Enactments in the clinical experience provide powerful insights into some developmental or clinical truths. In addition, enactments open the way for a new way of experiencing, seeing, listening, and understanding. In this film, experiences between characters surprise them and allow new ways of seeing, feeling and thinking about the self and others.

Finally, my way of using films offers new ways of teaching psychoanalytic process and concepts. By closely monitoring the film or film clips, all participant viewers involved in this shared material can learn about his or her unique contributions and reactions to the material, as well as study concepts such as fetish, transitional phenomena, screen memories, traumatic loss and intrapsychic effects and factors that facilitate change.

Exploring What is Curative

The Australian film *"Proof"* directed by Jocelyn Moorhouse, provides an excellent vehicle for exploring psychic change and the healing process. The dialectic between the relationship and the interpretation has been widely discussed, starting with Freud and Ferenczi, and continuing throughout the history of psychoanalysis. This film poignantly offers an opportunity to study the impact of spoken words, the manner in which they are spoken, and the insights and meanings signified by the words. An examination of this film sheds light on the nature of relationships and of interpretations that facilitate the creation of psychic space so that a person is able to see and experience in a new way—is able to give up pathological defenses and recover split-off parts of the self. In this way psychic development can resume and healthier relationships are possible.

In this study the significance of the camera and photographs as both transitional objects/phenomena and as fetish is discussed. Although Greenacre and others have studied similarities and differences between the two in depth, I am not aware of any previous mention that one object at different times may function as either fetish or transitional object.

Psychic Reality, Real Relationships and Memory

The manifest content of this film concerns Martin, a blind photographer, camera slung over his shoulder, in his journey in life after the traumatic childhood loss of his mother. Martin takes photographs with a camera he asked his mother to give him at age 10, when he knew he was going to lose her. He has people describe his photos so that he can recognize them later by a label he prints out in braille. But there is one photograph from his past that he has locked in his safe and has shown no one.

At age 32, he lives with his dog, Bill. His beautiful, seductive housekeeper, Celia (played by Genevieve Picot), is in love with him—is obsessed with him. She is intent on making him need her by consistently attending to his requests, and also by putting obstacles in his path and tricking him. Her intent is to make him feel less secure in being independent. He is contemptuous of her and intent on rejecting her. He disdains her sexual advances so that he can have the upper hand.

Flashbacks of himself with his mother depict the harsh inner image of mother and his anger at her that are frozen in his mind's eye since she left him. This is played out in his relationship with Celia.

What is the meaning of Martin's camera, always hanging on his shoulder? The camera and photographs may be viewed as a fetish that stands for the missing other, (the lost loved object, as well as the fantasied endangered phallus), yet also denies that the other is missing–denies that his mother is dead. Both Bronstein (1991) and Greenacre (1968) discuss the fetish as paradoxically undoing the separation from mother through a concrete substitute, while creating the illusion of being separate and independent. Martin reassures himself of his strength, independence, and manliness by using the camera. According to Greenacre (1968), "The denial of the actually witnessed injury can be met only by the use of a tangible, visible, and non-destructive part, which is the fetish. As in the case of most defenses, however, the fetish often contains direct or symbolic relics of the originally overwhelming situation."

Greenacre further states, "Certainly, there is an increase in sadomasochistic behavior in all perversions." According to Bronstein (1992), Sperling and Bak, the pre-genital fetish undoes the separation from mother through clinging to a concrete substitute.

Chasseguet-Smirgel (1985) adds that the male child's painful realization of his inadequacies to satisfy his mother are additional causes for the development of such a fetish. "As an omnipotent control is carried out on the fetish, the subject can bring it close up to him just as well as he can reject it, thus mastering all kinds of loss" (p. 88). This film highlights that it is not just inadequate mothering nor the smallness of the child, which contribute to the development of such a fetish, but the experience of trauma, deprivation and loss due to fate, such as congenital blindness, absence of a father, and death of a mother.

In the beginning of the film, Martin meets Andy (portrayed by Russell Crowe), who describes himself as the black sheep of his family [his mother thought he was lazy and would never amount to anything]. Martin likes Andy's style, and asks him to describe the photos he takes. Martin's impressive ability to know through smell, sound and touch is his check on whether Andy is telling him the truth. Upon Martin's finding Andy, a new function of the camera and photos becomes possible. They now serve as transitional objects that facilitate both connecting to the other and separating from him. Martin senses something different can happen with Andy and reaches out to him asking for help, using his photographs to initiate a journey guided by this new friend. Andy agrees to describe photographs that Martin takes in the present.

The function of the camera changes from that of fetish or talisman, which magically allays anxiety, to transitional object to promote growth through separation/individuation. Greenacre and others delineate the difference between fetish and transitional object. What is new in my analysis of the movie is that the same object can have multiple functions, depending in large part on the context and person in which it is employed—whether alone, in the company of Celia, or with Andy. This has implications for psychoanalytic technique. How the analyst allows the analysand to use objects, words or experiences is of great importance. The transference may be used either as fetish (Reed) or as a kind of transitional experience that opens up new perspectives and new choices.

In this film, Martin has two guides: Andy, who is honest, open, direct, curious, interested in Martin as a separate person; and, Celia, who is devious, manipulative, controlling, infantilizing, overprotective, and possessive. Celia interprets the photos so as to bind Martin to her and to seduce and attract him. With her, the photos are fetish, which protect him while he is connecting with the dangerous, bad untrustworthy mother. Celia has her own camera and photos by which she unconsciously possesses and controls Martin. The second guide, Andy, is honest, direct, guileless, emotionally responsive and connected. He is fascinated and comfortable with Martin, and is not afraid of his angry abrasive manner, nor of his blindness (a metaphor, perhaps, for vulnerability). Andy is amused and enjoys Martin in a way that Martin is not yet able to enjoy himself. When Martin shows his new friend Andy his pictures, his creative products are reflected as marvelous in Andy's admiring eyes. The photographs become transitional objects, in his connection to Andy. They now provide a bridge for both connecting and separating.

Winnicott emphasizes the importance of transitional objects and techniques over the years. "Out of these transitional phenomena develop much of what we variously allow and greatly value under the heading of religion and art..."

Thus Andy offers Martin a new possibility for development and psychic change. Martin's camera and picture taking acquire a new meaning, more in keeping with a transitional object and phenomenon. The camera is mother's eyes, an object that is mother, while at the same time an object that is not mother and allows him to be independent. According to Greenacre, "The transitional object, whatever is so chosen, is the tangible symbol of a relationship undergoing change. To some [people] it may be an ingredient of mourning." (Greenacre (1970, p.352). For Martin, the journey with Andy opens up the inner vision to experience sadness at the loss of his mother and to finally mourn.

Although Greenacre describes a continuum from fetish to transitional object, she clearly separates the two phenomena. In my view, this film demonstrates that the same object(s)—in this case the camera and photographs—can acquire new functions in the course of development, and may for a period of time, even shift back and forth between these two functions, in this case that of fetish and that of transitional object. When it is fetish (with Celia), the individual is a victim in a hostile world, rejecting reality and projecting pain. When it is the transitional object (with Andy) he is containing and working over painful reality and feelings of loss. He is the agent of his own life and resumes his capacity for play, for illusion, and for creativity. The fetish helps to maintain the status quo equilibrium, the developmental arrest, and is associated with concrete thinking; the transitional object helps to promote emotional development and separation/individuation. It also facilitates the development of symbolic thinking.

Martin had a very special attachment to his mother—she was his eyes, interpreting the world to him. When he was 10, she died; but he consciously believed that she abandoned him due to her shame and anger over his blindness, and unconsciously because of his desire for her and anger at her. In several flashbacks he remembers her. In the first flashback, we see Martin as a little boy coming upon his mother who is sleeping. He touches her face, her neck, her chest, her breasts ... and he remembers her awakening and harshly saying, "Martin, what are you doing? I've told you—you can't touch people whenever you want. Fingers are not the same as eyes. It's rude."

Martin's housekeeper, Celia, is paradoxically scheming, calculating, seductive, and nurturing. She catches Martin off-guard by appearing when not expected, and by placing obstacles in his path so that he will trip. Still, he feels he has the upper hand because she loves him, and he deprives her of the sexual, romantic relationship she desires with him.

The flashback of mother's sexual rejection occurs in association to his putting his hand over Celia's eyes so that she could not see the combination to his safe when he opens it to pay her. Touching Celia and covering her eyes reminds him of not being able to enjoy touching or gazing upon his mother. The oedipal prohibition simultaneously becomes the barrier to knowing his own desire, which at age 32 he disavows. Clearly the phallic meaning of fingers, and blindness as castration, play a part in Martin's psychic structure, and in this context the camera may be seen as a fetish which reassures that he can see, penetrate, and take the object he chooses to focus on (no pun intended). Although this is no doubt a factor, primary in this man's life are his issues with traumatic loss and separation/individuation.

Thus, we see Martin in the present with Celia in a sadomasochistic relationship in which Martin is enacting his belief of his relationship with mother—his psychic reality. This relationship represents a constant oscillation between nurturance and caring, and punishment and torturing, each role being alternately taken by Celia and Martin.

Although he uses Celia to describe his pictures (before meeting Andy) he does not trust that she is telling him the truth—just as he knows that she puts obstacles in his path to humiliate him and make him feel helpless and dependent upon her. Because he does not trust her description of the photos, her version of reality, her words and interpretation of the photos are not avenues of exploration or illumination, both emotionally and intellectually, but rather vehicles that prove he is independent and safe from Celia, while still needing her. His attachment to Celia is one of disavowal and alienation rather than one of warmth, nurturance and fun. Such an attachment to Celia precludes growth and joy, such an attachment to an analyst results in a negative therapeutic effect.

The next flashback shows Martin as a young boy listening to mother describing what's beyond the glass window, overlooking the garden. Mother tells him that in the garden there is a man raking leaves. Martin says he cannot hear leaves being raked and angrily insists: "He is not there, he was never there." Mother says: "Why would I lie to you?" and Martin replies, "Because you can." (The implication here is that people cannot be trusted. If you are blind, you are at the mercy of the person who describes the visual world to you.) This flashback occurs in association with the scene in which he asks his new friend, Andy, to describe the photos he takes. After

Andy agrees to do this on a regular basis, Martin warns, "You must *never lie* to me, Andy." Andy responds, "Why would I lie to you?"

The third flashback occurs after Celia blackmails him by taking a photo of him while he is on the toilet. She thereby forces him to spend an evening with her and surprises him by taking him to a symphony concert with her. During the concert, he is deeply moved; he takes off his glasses and puts his hand on his chest to feel his own heartbeat. At this moment, he can use his other senses, let himself know profoundly and creatively, rather than in a rigid, controlling, guarded and magical way through his photos as fetish and his sadomasochistic orientation. Celia takes him home, feeds him his favorite foods and starts to make love to him. He panics and blurts out, "You're not the only one, and runs out of her house."

He goes home and weeps, and spontaneously recalls his mother (who was clearly the only one) telling him that she's going to die: "I'll be sick and won't be able to look after you. I won't be able to describe the garden anymore. You have to live with Grandma." And Martin answers angrily: "You don't want to see me anymore. You're going to die to get away from me. You're ashamed of me. You're not telling the truth. You never do. I don't believe you!" The scene shifts to Martin as an angry little boy, tapping the coffin and saying, "It's hollow."

No doubt a life without her was hollow and unbearable. So he was convinced she had lied to him and was still alive. Arlow (1966) discussed that the defenses of depersonalization and derealization appear when the person is confronted by a danger he cannot master.

"By a process of denial in fantasy, and displacement, the individual is reassured that the danger is not real; besides, it is not happening to me." As Wolfenstein (1969) states, "For immature individuals the loss of a parent is also an intolerable injury to their fantasied omnipotence .... I interpret the repeated self-induced suffering of further losses as an unsuccessful effort to reassert this omnipotence. The compounding of narcissistic injury with object loss makes it more difficult to become reconciled to the loss."

The narcissistic injury of his blindness, the overdependence on his mother as his eyes, his rage at her for his blindness, the shameful discovery and painful rejection by his mother when he tried to explore, understand and

91

enjoy her body with his hands, and her leaving him forever by dying resulted in his clinging to his omnipotence, denying the reality of her death, developing a sado-masochistic orientation to life, and denying both her and his own helplessness in the face of her tragic illness and his blindness. He called her a liar, and interpreted her loving acts as hateful ones, believing her grooming his hair meant she was ashamed to be seen in public with him at the barbers. He lied to himself; his psychic reality was thus formed.

The narcissistic Celia perpetuated Martin's overdependence, while Andy respected and had faith in Martin's ability to be independent, using the photos to foster this. The implication for a therapeutic analytic stance recognizes the humiliation of adults seeking help and becoming dependent as a child on the analyst, and the need to be helped to maintain one's independent power while still seek the help. This is Andy's forte as enabler.

Even as trust was developing with Andy, Martin still resisted some of Andy's interpretation. Thus when Andy spontaneously described a photo he saw on Martin's mantelpiece as depicting Martin's mother, looking quite pale, sitting on a park bench, her arm around his shoulder, he could not revise his belief that his mother was ashamed to be seen in public with him. Martin could not yet use Andy's interpretation to revise his beliefs about mother—could not yet change his psychic reality about his mother and himself in relation to her. Nor did Andy insist on it. He was still not strong enough to accept and mourn their love for each other, as well as his profound loss. He still clung to the unconscious belief of the rejecting mother—paradoxically embedded a magical hope that his mother is still alive, and not really gone forever. Through this belief, he could preserve his magical omnipotence—i.e. it was both his fault that his mother left him. and his mother is always with him in hatred. Martin's inability to use interpretations until he was ready is similar to what happens in the analytic situation.

In some ways, time stopped for Martin after mother's death, and his heart became frozen. The reality of mother's death was unthinkable, and he denied it. According to Loewald (1980), when the lost object is not mourned, internalization does not occur, and external substitutes are sought. This film demonstrates that the nature of the substitutes reflects the psychic reality of the subject. Martin's internal self-mother relationship is externalized in his substitute relationship with Celia, his use of the camera as fetish, and his turning passive into active. Instead of desiring and enjoying touching Celia's breasts, as had been his wish with mother, he rejects Celia's invitation for sexual pleasure, feeling powerful and pitying her, the one who desires and is frustrated and deprived. Martin's psychic reality of mother as being at once nurturing, cold, controlling, seductive, deceptive, and cruel is enacted in his relationship with Celia.

With Celia, Martin turned passive into active. Instead of desiring and enjoying touching her breasts, as had been his wish with mother, he rejects Celia's invitation for sexual pleasure. He now feels powerful and pities Celia, while she is the one whose desires are frustrated and deprived.

Andy and Martin

From the start, Andy responded to Martin from his own perspective, but could also recognize that Martin could have a different perspective, a different psychic reality. Andy is nurturing, yet separate, and creatively opens up new horizons for Martin without guilt. Celia also opens up new horizons for Martin, but with humiliation, trickery and strings attached. Andy really enjoys Martin and is amused by him. Celia is obsessed with him. She is constricted by a theory of the needy, helpless Martin, whereas Andy treats him like a regular guy. Yet, Celia's awakening his senses and sensual pleasure, along with Andy's friendship and words were no doubt instrumental in his getting in touch with his grief and bereavement.

After observing Martin accidentally bump into crates which fall on a cat, Andy accused Martin of killing the cat—a metaphor for Andy's intuitive insight into Martin's rage, and his own depressive, negative orientation in life. Martin then expressed his tenderness and faith by taking the cat into his arms, saying "He's not dead." Although for Andy, the cat was dead, he could also understand that to Martin the cat was alive—that they had different perceptions. They went together to the veterinarian to find out which it was. Martin took photographs in the waiting room and asked Andy to help him angle the camera so he could capture the images he sought.

The next day, he went to Andy, asking him to describe the photos, photos which amazingly captured both the characters of the people, their pets, and their relationship to each other in a humorous way. Andy's words about the present events and photos penetrated and pleased Martin since there was also room for Martin's words to be heard. Words in a social context create new meaning (Vigotsky), whereas words with no listeners keep the speaker stuck and trapped in a closed system. The camera and photos, as transitional objects, open doors for separation and connectedness. Eventually, the dialogue between Andy and Martin, and the experiences they shared opened up new insights and allowed for a revision of old inner pictures. This became possible both through transference enactments, the real relationship, and words describing present and past pictures (i.e. interpretations).

Andy is truly interested in learning more about Martin. Without fear, he says what others only think "That's weird. A blind photographer. Don't get me wrong; it's good you're doing something creative." Martin explains that his mother gave him the camera when he was 10 years old. Empathetically, Andy replies, "That was cruel of her." Martin corrects him, saying that he asked his mother for the camera, thinking it would help him to see. However, it is not until much later that Martin can use the information that he gave to Andy as proof that his mother was not cruel. Although he told Andy, "No, don't think my mother was cruel," he himself could not believe otherwise; the words and the beliefs and emotions were not concordant. Similarly, he could not take in Andy's interpretation of the picture of himself and mother in the park, still insisting that mother cut his hair to avoid being seen in public with him. This is similar to the analytic situation in which the analysand relates memories before being able to integrate them into a meaningful emotional context and hears interpretations before being able to consciously benefit from them. The analyst, Andy, serves as a container, keeping the words of Martin, the secrets not yet recognized consciously for future shared discovery. He hears the resistance and accepts it, recognizing that Martin cannot yet see differently.

Martin tells Andy, "I took my first picture when I was 10....just a garden visible from one of the windows in our flat, but the most important photo I've ever taken. Every morning and every afternoon my mother would describe this garden to me. I saw the seasons come and go through her eyes. I would question her so thoroughly, trying to catch her in a lie. I never did, but by taking the photo I knew that I could one day." To Andy's question as to why his mother would lie to him, Martin replied, "To punish me for being blind."

Andy initiates Martin to moving pictures in a drive-in movie theater. Martin leaves his own camera and still photos at home, trusting Andy to give him truthful descriptions of the pictures and the action on the screen. The movie within the movie provides a means for Martin to rediscover fantasy and lively passions of desire and rage. Andy, like the good-enough analyst, has created a space that is safe for Martin to express his murderous rage at the beautiful, seductive, sexual woman—the mother who, in Andy's case, was critical and demeaning, and in Martin's case, who deprived him of eyesight to enjoy looking at her, and of physically enjoying touching her, and who he was so unbearably dependent upon and desirous of, and who abandoned him when he was 10 by dying.

Andy describes an attractive woman on the screen who is bare breasted with perky nipples and about to be attacked by a man with a knife. Martin confides in Andy, "If you analyze your feelings, you really want the killer to get the girl," and the two men bond around desire and rage at the sexual woman. This may be seen as a beginning in the process of separation from the taboo oedipal mother, a task of adolescence neither man had completed before this. Just before the cut to this scene, Martin was telling Andy that he hates Celia, but keeps her on and rejects her so that he can have pity on her. He is stuck, so far unable to let go of his attachment through hate and enacting it in his relationship with Celia.

The awakening of Martin's adolescent curiosity about the world and growing interest in his own sexuality and masculine identity is suggested when he is alone in the car in the drive-in, after Andy leaves to buy some food. He slides over to the driver's seat, finds condoms in Andy's car, and holds them up to the side window, reminiscent of his holding up his hands to the windowpane when he was a child. Once again in this film, the window glass with hands up against it is portrayed as something interesting yet frustrating and puzzling to Martin. What does it represent? The incest barrier? Or the barrier that he feels between his inner true self and the external world that he feels shut out from? Glass can be seen through, but if vision is not possible, then it represents a barrier that protects but also limits. His explorations are observed by the man in the next car, who threateningly calls Martin a fag. Martin's question, "Are you addressing me?" is heard as "Are you undressing me?" Clearly, not only gestures, but also words are misinterpreted based on the psychic reality of the subject. In this case, the stranger projects his homosexual desires onto Martin.

Further bonding between Andy and Martin occurs when Andy risks his own safety to defend Martin. Here the guide/friend/therapeutic agent introduces him into an exciting, dangerous world, separates from him in order to nourish him, attacks his attackers, and invites him to stay in the driver's seat and be in control of the phallic vehicle as they drive away and escape from their attackers. The paradoxical role of Andy is strikingly clear in this vignette, and analogous to the paradoxical role of the analyst. They crash, and Martin fabricates a story to the police that the accident made him blind. When the doctor discovers that Martin's blindness is congenital, and wonders how he could be driving, he tells her: "I forgot." The two men laugh hilariously afterwards about this escapade, and about their lies.

At this moment, the concept of lying is beginning to shift in Martin's psyche, occupying a more flexible, benign, playful space. The new experience in the drive-in movie theater and in the driver's seat in the car with Andy pave the way for a new way of seeing himself. That is as someone who can and does lie for fun and protection, and someone who can forget that he is blind (i.e. vulnerable) and can sit in the driver's seat with pleasure. The new experiences may best be understood as "informative experiences," as described by Judith Chused (1996). In this paper, she asserts and demonstrates that before a patient can use an interpretation for psychic change, his perceptual frame must change, a process that is rarely initiated by the verbal content of an interpretation alone. Instead, alterations in perception usually require experiences which are discordant with expectations. Renik has written that enactments are indeed necessary ingredients of any psychotherapeutic change.

Thus, Andy's fighting the humiliators of Martin resulted in their both surviving the trauma and danger of male aggressiveness. It was a step in Martin's being freed from being a victim. They both become joyful and victorious, playfully joking about their adventure, their illusions, and their lies to the authorities.

The relationship of Andy and Martin develops poignantly. Martin tells Andy he trusts him, and Andy says, "Maybe you shouldn't. I'm not good at responsibility. My boss, my parents, think I'm useless. If you could see me, you'd agree!" i.e. that, "I, too, am handicapped." The implication here is that Martin's blindness prevents Martin from seeing the truth about Andy. Martin sees Andy as competent, strong, spontaneous, gentle, fun and protective; Andy sees Martin as powerful, accomplished, competent, vulnerable, curious, better than him. They both are also not frightened by each other's flaws and vulnerabilities. Like the good enough mother, and the good enough analyst, they are able to take in each other's spontaneous gestures, give them reality and meaning through spoken words, and make sense of them.

Martin, for the first time in this film can laugh. In the absence of the camera as fetish, the process of internalization and symbolization here is evident. The two men play and enjoy an illusion they have created. They become open to new ideas and experiences. Psychic space has opened up within each of them and between them so that psychic reality can be changed. Through both a new experience and words spoken in a safe relationship this became possible.

I see this as parallel to the psychoanalytic situation. The analyst in the course of opening up potential space for play between and within each participant in the analytic journey is herself changed in the process and by the process, even though, as was the case with Andy, the focus is primarily in understanding and helping the analysand. The analysand is also relatively "blind" to some of the weaknesses of the analyst, and in the transference, the analyst can grow as well.

The blissful union between Martin and Andy is shattered soon afterward when Martin discovers that Andy lied to him to protect Celia. He goes home to find Celia and Andy making love, and enraged, he kicks them both out. The fantasy that he is the only loved one for both Andy and Celia has been undone, and he is painfully disappointed. Just as in analysis, the analyst must frustrate oedipal yearnings. Martin is betrayed and lied to by both

Celia and Andy. The symbiotic tie with mother as portrayed in his memories and enacted with Celia is jarred. They are now three.

At this point in the movie, Martin is able to let in the experience of desire for his mother, and also open to his awareness and sadness about losing her. This is portrayed by a visit to the cemetery the following day, under the true light of a clear blue sky. He finds out that indeed his mother is buried there; she did not lie; she did die in the year that he was 10. Martin's facing his mother's death and mourning her and his own helplessness and rage enable him to revise his memories and inner representations of self and mother. He now can say goodbye to Celia, the sadistic imago of his mother, and masochistic representation of himself. He becomes tender and gentle with Celia, yet strong, apologizing for tormenting her for so long. "I knew how you felt about me. It was wrong of me to exploit your feelings." He lets her go with compassion and firmness. This is an important clue that his psychic reality has undergone significant changes.

Andy returns after a period of estrangement to tell Martin he has changed, he is now more industrious, working 2 shifts and saving money to start a mail order business. The analogy of the analyst as well as the analysand growing as a result of the psychoanalytic process is drawn. Andy's growth resulted from his interest and curiosity about Martin, who impressed him as a fighter determined to get what he wants, who was handicapped yet struggling to be heard and appreciated, a fiercely independent man who was making his way in the world. Andy could see beyond Martin's bitterness to his life force (although Andy thought the cat to be dead, Martin saw he was alive and took him to the vet). Andy appreciated Martin's humor and intelligence, as well as his enjoyment of literature and music.

In his interaction with Martin, Andy discovered untapped strengths within himself to communicate and be taken in, since Martin appreciated his style, describing it as simple and direct. Andy felt recognized by Martin who did not judge or stereotype him. Andy was inspired to give more to Martin than he was initially asked to do, to open up discussion about conflict and contradiction, to enter into new territory, at once thrilling emotionally, nurturing, dangerous and potentially painful. He risked being both assertive and yielding with Martin. Through this journey with Martin, he, too, found a true self that had been locked away. So, too, the analyst finds new ways of being heard, seen and experienced that reciprocally lead to new ways of being in the journey with their analysands. For it is impossible for the analyst to impact upon the analysand without the reciprocal impact upon the analyst. As Andre Green (source not remembered) poetically said, no analysis is meaningful without both the analyst and the analysand at some point crying.

The difference between an analytic relationship and a movie is, of course, that in the latter the character representing the therapeutic role is in sharper and more dramatic focus. Although there are always enactments in analysis itself, they are on a much subtler level. Through Andy's journey with Martin, he learns to use words, to question, to revise, to connect, bridge and interpret, while at the same time allowing space for Martin's defenses, and time for his ego to strengthen. Through this journey, Andy's ego became stronger as well. Furthermore, Andy's own oedipal resolution is portrayed through his enactment of desire and betrayal with Celia, a woman like his mother, who does not value him in his own right, only caring for Martin. This is shown in the movie when he goes to Celia's apartment and is horrified to see that her walls are lined with photographs that she has taken of Martin. He walks out on her. Martin's anger and rejection of him (in the context of their loving relationship), and Andy's ability to reject Celia once he learns he is not loved by her, enable him to separate and grow stronger.

Upon Andy's return, Martin takes off his glasses to intimately communicate with Andy and berates him for lying to him. "You can't know how important truth is to me." Andy, in a moving speech, replies, "Shit, everybody lies, but not all the time, and that's the point. I lied to you about Celia. That was the only time." Martin asks, "How can I believe you?" "You can't," says Andy. "You tell the truth, Martin. Your whole life's the truth." With this statement, Andy confronts an important truth about Martin. As Winnicott (1960) states, "These recognitions of important fact, made clear at the right moments, pave the way for communication with the true self." (p.152) Absolute certainty and absolute trust are never possible in reality. Learning to mourn and forgive failures in self and loved ones are therapeutic.

At that moment, it seems very likely that Martin was able to question if he had lied to himself for the last 22 years, secreting away his treasured connection to his mother and the father within him. For twenty years he

99

kept his secret, the picture he took of the garden which could someday either prove or disprove that his mother lied to him about the presence of a man in the garden.

Through the continued words and relationship with Andy, the trust had been built up, destroyed and then repaired. He was at last able to tolerate knowing the truth, including his own defensive need to lie to himself. He unlocks the cherished secret, the photo of the garden that he has kept hidden in his safe since he was 10 and shows it to Andy. Andy describes a kind, old man in the garden, the final proof that mother was not a liar. The implication here is that even someone like Martin who has such acute hearing, can tune out sounds such as the man raking in the garden, either out of anxiety or desire. Up until now, Martin had refused to believe the reality of a man in the garden, perhaps wanting to believe that he was the only man in mother's eyes, and also that mother was not missed because she was a liar.

Why did Martin keep the important photograph secret all these years? Kahn (1983) discusses one function of a secret. His patient, Carolyn, buried (hid) the candlesticks associated with a happy time with mother, after she lost her special connection with mother. She became detached, as if the happy connection to herself as well was also buried. According to Kahn, she had absented herself into a secret when her ongoing life with her mother broke down. She gradually recovered this part of herself during her analysis and could dig up the candlesticks.

Perhaps Martin absented his loving connection with his mother in his secret when he lost her but could later share the secret with a new love object who both nurtured him, understood him, cared about him, failed him and returned wanting to share the positive impact that Martin had on his life. Until then, Martin could not remember his mother's enjoyment of him, the positive impact he had on her life, but could only remember how dependent he was on her when she left him. Perhaps Martin's secret was his way of creating a potential space, a kind of bank account to draw on at some unknown future date when it could be used. According to Kahn "... a person can hide himself into symptoms or he can absent himself into a secret. Here, the secret provides a potential space where an absence is sustained in suspended animation.

The secret carries the hope that one day the person will be able to emerge out of it, be found and met, and then become a whole person, sharing life with others" (p.105). "Clinically, it is only if we succeed in gradually creating an atmosphere of mutuality with these patients that they can share their secret with us. This sharing of the experience amounts to that 'experience of mutuality' that is the essence of the mother's capability to adapt to the baby's need. What had enabled Carolyn to share her secret was my capacity to contain and hold all the confusion and risk her behavior perpetrated inside and outside the analysis over the first eight months..."(p106). What had enabled Martin to share his secret was Andy's capacity to contain and hold all the confusion in communication and behavior in his relationship with Martin. Andy had succeeded in creating an atmosphere of mutuality and authentic respect for Martin as a separate person. Moreover, he truly enjoyed Martin.

Through Andy's and Celia's help, including Andy's finding a lovable mother in Celia, Martin rediscovers his loving trust in his mother. He can begin to accept that she had another man in her life, represented in Martin's psychic reality by the gardener, and to accept that she did die. Upon relinquishing his omnipotent quest for perfect loyalty, truth, and control, he experiences profound sadness. He now recovers a memory of himself at 10, being alone in the room overlooking the garden. He is touching the pane of glass. It is raining outside, but birds are singing. There is once again life and the possibility of joy as well as profound sorrow.

Conclusion

Martin's sado-masochistic orientation to life had provided a defense both against accepting his losses and mourning them, as well as facing his desire for, and rage at his mother. The sadomasochism was a magical solution that froze his emotional development and deprived him of the real pleasures of sex and love. The camera and photos functioned at different times as fetish or transitional objects and phenomena. With Celia, the photos and camera served as a fetish, protecting him by freezing time, and providing a means of both showing and protecting himself, when in the company of she who he needed, but did not trust. With Andy he used his photos as transitional objects for connecting and separating, and to learn to trust. By the end of the movie, Martin's psychic reality had changed; he could finally see, enabled by Andy's entrance into his life, which created two dyadic relationships and a triangle.

Both Andy's words and his experiences with Andy (enactments) organize Martin's inner and outer reality. Martin develops compassion for himself and Celia. Andy reflected, clarified and interpreted Martin's world of photographs, as well as introduced him into new experiences. His self-expressions facilitated Martin's identifying with him as well as separating from him. Martin is then able to let go of Celia, the hateful representation of mother and self, marking an important step in mourning his loss and reconstructing his past. His love with Celia was an entrapping sado-masochistic bondage.

His bond with Andy was both loving and competitive, expanding each other's worlds. After first experiencing adventure and joyful illusion with Andy, as well as revealing interpretations of his photos and his relationship with his mother, and then betrayal and disillusionment with Andy Martin began to relinquish his omnipotence. His brittle defenses had lifted, and hope and a future were re-found. He now had the ego strength to both re-find his love for his mother, and to mourn her loss and to separate from her.to both re-find his love for his mother, and to mourn her loss and to separate from her.

REFERENCES

ARLOW, J. A. (1966) Depersonalization and Derealization in Psychoanalysis: Clinical Theory and Practice, Madison, Connecticut: International University Press, (1991), pp. 137-154.

BRONSTEIN, A. (1992.) The Fetish, Transitional Objects an Illusion., Psych Rev, Vol 79, #2. pp.

CHASSEGUET-SMIRGEL, J. (1985) Creativity and Perversion, New York & London: W.W. Norton & Co.

Chused, J., (1996) The Therapeutic Action of Psychoanalysis Abstinence and Informative Experiences, JAPA, Vol 44, #4, pp1047

Greenacre, P. (1969). The Fetish and the Transitional Object. in "Emotional Growth", Vol I. New York: International Universities Press, (1971), pp. 315-334.

-------(1970) The Transitional Object and the Fetish: With Special Reference to the Role of Illusion, in "Emotional Growth", Vol I. New York: International Universities Press, (1971), pp. 335-352.

KHAN, M.M.R. (1983) Secret as Potential Space (p97-107) in "Hidden Selves". Madison, Connecticut: International University Press, pp.97-107.

LOEWALD, H.W. (1980) Internalization, Separation, Mourning, and the Superego, P. 257-276, in Papers on Psychoanalysis, New Haven and London: Yale University Press, pp.257-276.

RENIK, O.,WINNICOTT, D.W., (1960) Ego Distortion in Terms of True and False Self, in The Maturational Processes and the Facilitating

Environment, New York: International University Press, Inc., pp.140-152.

------ (1988)   Human Nature, New York: Schocken Books.

WOLFENSTEIN, M. (1969) Loss, Rage and Repetition, in Psychoanalytic Study of the Child, V24, New York: International University Press, pp. 432-460.

VIGOTSKY, L.S. (1934), Thought and Speech, in Language and Thought, Chapter VII, Moscow, USSR: Grosisdat.

CHAPTER SEVEN ଔ

Lust, Caution
Directed by Ang Lee (2007)

Passion and Politics: Personal Dangers of Collaboration and Resistance

Lust, Caution—a provocative title—and one that apparently puts off would-be movie goers, because it was not a box office success. Is it the juxtaposition of an invitation to indulge and enjoy raw and intense sexuality with the admonition that such an enjoyment can be dangerous? Is it that people don't want to know about contradictions and complications that comprise the reality of their inner world and the reality of the world in which they grew up and currently live?

Introduction

Lust, Caution is both a historical movie, taking place in the 1930's when China was occupied by the Japanese, and a study of the passions, fears and personal traumas of the people who lived during this period of Chinese history. Ang Lee, the director (whose other movies include *Brokeback Mountain*, *Crouching Tiger, Hidden Dragon*, *Life of Pi*, *Eat Drink Man Woman*, and *The Ice Storm*) sensitively illuminates the complex psychology of both the collaborator and the militant resistor. They are portrayed, not as unidimensional members of a group, but as individuals, each with his or her own unique psychology. Moreover, there is a cultural context that adds another dimension to the experiences and outcomes for all the individuals in the movie.

Ang Lee hones-in on the passions of love and hatred, on the awakening of intense sexual desire, and the unleashing of brutal murderous aggression. This is not a movie of "good guys" and "bad guys". Perhaps this is another reason *Lust, Caution* has not received the popularity and viewer interest that I feel it deserves. Ang Lee shows us both the vulnerabilities, fears, and intense loving passions of the collaborators, and the traitors of their country, as well their greed, sadism, and quest for power. And he shows us the vulnerabilities, the passionate love of country, but fear of loving intimacy among the members of the underground resistance movement.

We are helped to understand that the collaborators, the betrayers of their own people, have done it for power and money; and that those who join the resistance movement are loyal, caring, and brave, and idealistically want to fight in the underground to kill the collaborators. In fact, we come to understand that the collaborators are even more hateful and despicable than the conquerors (the Japanese), because they are traitors betraying their very own people.

There are also two love stories that parallel the political story. One is tender, painfully shy, fearful, and unrequited, and the other is initially sadistic and hateful, evolving into an overwhelmingly passionate lustful exploration of each other's physical and emotional being, a deeply moving love/hate relationship that throws caution to the winds.

Discussion

A young college student, Wong Chia Chi (played by Tong Wei), spends the summer with other students in an acting group. Her mother had recently died; her father has moved to England with her brother, leaving her behind, and soon afterwards marrying. Wong Chia Chi is naïve, impressionable, emotionally open and enraptured with old romantic movies. As she watches the movie she weeps, both in identification with the character in the movie, as well as for her own recent losses of mother and father. There is instant "chemistry" between her and the handsome young director of the acting school, Kuang Yu Min (portrayed by Wang Leehom). Wong Chia Chi auditions for a patriotic play that was meant to raise money for the resistance movement. She demonstrates an exquisite capacity for conveying a depth and breadth of emotions that clearly impresses and excites Kuang immensely. He selects her to be the lead actor opposite him. When the play is enacted, the Chinese audience is enthralled with the performances, especially hers, and with her final tearful, passionate words, *"China will not fall!"*

Five of the young actors decide to form a resistance plan to kill one of the chief Chinese collaborators, Mr. Yee (played by Tony Leung Chiu-wai), and they ask her to join them. The plan is that Wong Chia Chi will befriend Mr. Yee's wife (Joan Chen), join their afternoon mahjong game, and in that way find an entry to connecting with the husband, collaborator, Mr. Yee. But to do this they decide she must develop a persona of a married woman of the world. So as not to be "caught in the lie," they try to leave no stone unturned, she must not be a virgin. In the process of choosing the man to initiate her, she looks at the man she is very attracted to. But sadly, he cannot take on the invitation. Finally, one of the group says he knows how to do it, having once slept with a whore. The experience is clinical and painful for both of them.

When we next see Wong Chia Chi, she is transformed into a sophisticated, extremely beautiful, mysterious and enticing woman. Through befriending Mr. Yee's wife, she is able to be included in daily mahjong games. She then manages to meet with the collaborator, Mr. Yee, the intended victim. Wong Chia Chi takes him to her tailor and helps him select and fit beautiful stylish suits. Although clearly intrigued by her, he later resists her invitation to enter her home, obviously desiring her, but cautious about possible enemies who may be inside. After he leaves, his driver enters the young resistors' home, now suspecting their plot to kill his boss. After he pulls out a gun, they jump him, stab him numerous times in a horrible, bloody scene. The final killing is performed by Kuang, who grabs the dying man's head in his two hands and turns it around 180 degrees. The young man is horrified and deeply shaken by his own vicious, sadistic deed.

The group disbands, and we next see the young woman back in Shanghai, studying Japanese in order to get a job. She receives a letter from her father. He writes that he cannot afford to send for her. Now abandoned by her father, she has no choice but to remain in China. She meets the young director Kuang after three years of separation. He invites her to join a more professional resistance movement. The plan once again is for her to seduce the collaborator, Mr. Yee, so that his murder at last could be completed. Mr. Yee had advanced to a higher, more powerful position, and is now under immense protective guard. The leader of the resistance is a seasoned, hardened organizer, very unlike the idealistic young actor-resistors.

Abandoned by her father, she decides to accept the dangerous assignment of seducing "Mr. Yee" and then setting a trap for him to be killed.

The initial sexual encounter between Chia Chi and Mr. Yee is brutal. She is spunky and defiant, and he brutally shows her who is boss by ripping her pants, slapping and raping her as she gasps and screams. At their next encounter, she tells him "I hate you!" He thanks her for this, saying at last he can believe something that he is told. Over and over again she repeats "I hate you," and it begins to sound more like a feeling of love than of hate. We see here the very beginning of a transformation in these two people, who are both so different, yet alike. They each are on opposite sides of the political battle, but both are lonely and vulnerable, while also passionate and gutsy. She demands to be treated better the next time he tries to make a date with her, and the next encounter is more mutual, lustful and mutually passionate. Their encounters become more and more long-lasting, with two beautiful bodies exploring, intertwining, writhing, stroking, sucking, kissing—in some of the most passionate screen scenes and beautiful cinematography I have ever seen.

As Chia Chi feels herself becoming more and more emotionally involved with Mr. Yee, she urges the resistance leader to get on with the killing. "Shoot him while he's coming in me so that I can feel his brains and blood spilling all over me. Please do it before it's too late." It was at this last meeting, when a plan was being set up, that Kuang (her original love interest) grabbed her and kissed her passionately. She softly and sadly said, "You could have done that three years ago. Why didn't you?"

I believe the implication is that if he had the courage to be passionate, lustful, sexually and affectionately loving to her at that time, she would not have been so open to falling in love with the collaborator—a man whose lust and complicated, conflicted emotions spoke to her, stirring up both her lust and her love—as well as his own. Mr. Yee became for her the loving father—a substitute for the father who abandoned her after her mother died. For the young man, acting upon his aggression, though scary, was far less frightening than acting upon his lustful, loving feelings.

The collaborator gives Chia Chi an exquisite, dazzling diamond ring— clearly an expression of love—of symbolic marriage. The music before and during this scene is an extremely passionate, sexual, sensual, aggressive Argentine Tango.

The trap to kill Mr. Yee had been set up to occur at the time of the pickup of her ring. She puts the ring on, and he says the beauty is not in the ring but in the hand of she who is wearing it. She is clearly confused and shaken—then anxiously whispers to him, "Go now! Please go now!" He understands and runs for his life, literally leaping into the car that is waiting for them. He is saved; she is caught! When Mr. Yee's guard gives him the ring that Chia Chi has offered to return, he says, "It doesn't belong to me." Interestingly, he soon learns that his guards all knew or at least suspected him of this affair but did not report it—saying to him "Well, you were involved with her." I infer this to mean such an emotional involvement on the part of their boss overrode their political duties. He instructs his men to shoot all five members of this resistance plot, and in the last scene we see them kneeling at the edge of a huge dark, deep hole, the quarry. These five show emotions ranging from rage to sadness to confusion and forgiveness. And the face of the Mr. Yee also exhibits all of these mixed emotions.

This complex movie portrays young love and their fear of sex and intimacy with each other. It powerfully portrays rage at the betraying countryman, intertwined with rage at the betraying and abandoning father. Rage is intermixed with and followed by lustful encounters with this betrayer, who is also a father figure. It is significant that after Chia Chi learns of her father's final rejection of her, she agrees to the plan to have a sexual liaison with Mr. Yee. It is also significant that if only Kuang could have "kissed" her, been less afraid of consummation of his desires and acknowledging her desires for him, the story would have been very different. They could have had lives of their own, rather than live through a political mission of love of country and hatred of betrayers of them and their country.

CHAPTER EIGHT ෬

The Piano Teacher
Directed by Michael Haneke (2001)

Perversion Annihilates Creativity and Love: A Passion for Destruction in Haneke's "The Piano Teacher"[1]

Michael Haneke's film *The Piano Teacher* (2001) is a viscerally clenching and disturbing, dark cinematic portrayal of enmeshment, repression, sadism, masochism and destruction counterpointed by the soaring romantic music (composed by Martin Achenbach) that infuses the dramatic narrative. Carried out with artistic discretion and chilling reserve reminiscent of Jane Campion's *The Piano* (Allen 1995; Wrye 1998), *The Piano Teacher* dramatizes the excruciating strangulation of creative jouissance and vitality that psychic annihilation and perversion foster. *The Piano Teacher* is in vivid contrast to Roman Polanski's recent portrayal of pianist Wladyslaw Szpilman's tortured but successful struggles to avoid physical and psychic extermination in the Warsaw Ghetto through the transmuting power of his relationship to music. *The Piano Teacher* shows a life in which the exquisite humanism of the music that she plays and teaches cannot save her tormented soul.

---

[1] An earlier version of this chapter was presented Nov. I, 2003 in London at the Second European Psychoanalytic Film Festival (EPFF II), sponsored by the International Psychoanalytic Association and the British Psychoanalytical Society. It was one of a panel of papers with Alexander Stein and Diana Diamond, entitled "Exquisite Harmony, Silence and Traumatic Discord in *The Pianist* and *The Piano Teacher*.,,

This chapter was originally published in the International Journal of Psychoanalysis in December 15, 2003.

Underlying and informing the tight and conflicted characterization of Erika Kohut, the piano teacher, portrayed by Isabelle Huppert, lies the dark labyrinth of mother daughter bonds and bondage. *The Piano Teacher* explores dialectical tensions between dependency and autonomy, creativity and destructiveness, longing and deadness, innocence and sexual perversion, psychosis and repressive control. Symbolic of these dialectical tensions is the fact that most of the film's scenes are either set in formal, elegant and sophisticated settings evocative of the cultural and intellectual gatherings of Vienna such as the opening piano recital, or in raunchy, sordid settings—toilets, porn booths, locker rooms, evocative of the world of baser instincts.

The Viennese locale has particular reference for psychoanalysts: as we observe the tangled enmeshed relationship between mother and daughter driving the piano teacher to increasingly destructive furtive acts of self-loathing and rage, the film plays like a tour de France through one of Freud's lost case histories and offers us psychoanalytic film buffs rich fodder. Whether accidental or unconscious, the protagonist's name "Kohut" also evokes the psychoanalytic scion of empathic attunement, Heinz Kohut, and *empathic attunement is the crucial maternal attribute exquisitely lacking in this case history.*

Director Michael Haneke, known for Funny Games, his earlier study of claustrophobia and sadism (1997), is a master at delineating alienated, emotionally frigid individuals. He waited 15 years to take this adaptation of Elfriede Jelinek's 1983 novel to the screen, refusing to proceed without Isabelle Huppert whose formidable range allows her to traverse moment to moment between the pathetically vulnerable and the sharply intellectual. Critic Scott Tobias wrote, "Huppert controls every movement with frightening precision, wearing her face like an eggshell that sheaths her immense vulnerability." For her performance, she deservedly won the best actress prize at Cannes in 2001, and her co-star, Benoit Magimel, won the best actor award while the film itself won the grand jury prize.

Despite such accolades, *The Piano Teacher* has definitely proven too strong for some audiences though for those of us of a clinical bent, and more accustomed to close encounters with sadomasochism and derailments of desire, it provides a brilliant case history of the twisted impact of maternal intrusiveness and the perversion of narratives of desire.

Mother Daughter Bond or Bondage

Even before the opening scene of The Piano Teacher is over, we are exposed to the dynamics of the twisted relationship between Professor Erika Kohut (Isabelle Humbert) and her mother (Annie Girardot). Although conservatively dressed Erika, wearing no make-up and often twisting her hair into a tight bun, has her own room, she sleeps in a twin bed next to her mother in the master bedroom, communicating the extent to which both she and mother are tangled in pre-oedipal and oedipal drama. We learn that Erika's father, whose place she now occupies, has some time ago descended into madness and was institutionalized. Although only a couple of hours have passed since Erika gave her last piano lesson at Vienna's prestigious music conservatory, her fretful and domineering mother, with whom she shares the parental bedroom in an old apartment building, is concerned because she hasn't heard from her forty-something daughter.

In the opening scene, the intrusive mother, vividly portrayed with tense, steely fragility by Girardot, demands and ransacks her daughter's purse, a well-worn but nevertheless apt metaphor for her efforts to control her daughter's sexuality and also an icon for classical mythological depictions of the potency of the vengeful and furious Medusa-mother (Balter, 1969)). In the purse, she discovers her booty, Erika has purchased a frock ostensibly spending their rent money, Erika's earnings as a professor of music. In retaliation, Erika accuses mother of stealing her autumn suit, while reminding mother she once had a very similar designer frock. This scene illustrates Adrienne Harris's[2] observations on how female envy and passion can be so excruciatingly played out in women's rivalrous destructiveness in

---

[2] Adrienne Harris is on the faculty of NYU Post-Doctoral Program in Psychoanalysis and Psychotherapy

relation to each other's clothing (Harris, 1993; Kaplan 1991). Mother and daughter launch into each other with such harsh physicality and vitriol that Erika's new frock is ripped in the struggle and mother's scalp is cut; eventually the daughter crumples into guilty tears of submission, revealing the extent to which middle-aged Erika is still in bondage to her mother.

In this mother daughter dyad, maternal passion has been perverted into envious destructiveness and spoiling; symbolically the romantic music of Schumann and Schubert that Professor Erika Kohut is so famous for teaching is counterposed on the film soundtrack against the sounds of their raging cat fight and by the rasp of furniture being dragged across the floor to block passage of mother to daughter. What has happened here to extinguish the cooing and soothing sounds of an optimally attuned mother, containing and metabolizing her own and her child's anxieties?

Here instead, normal mother/child closeness which would optimally foster jouissance and passionate flowering, has collapsed into a rivalrous paranoid vacuum. (Wrye, 1996) Here, mother views daughter both as her own hated narcissistic extension, her puppet pianist and her own oedipal rival, conflating her daughter's capacity to separate and blossom. Mother sorely lacks appropriate boundaries and what Ceccoli calls "the dialectic between restraint and emotional accessibility" (2003) that is the hallmark of healthier relating. Defending against suffocation by her mother's control, permeated by projections of her mother's demeaned femininity and unable to turn to her absent father for protection and support (Elise, 1998), Erika turns to obsessional, schizoid and perverse defenses in her deformed erotic life and in her teaching.

From this very opening scene, we are given a dramatic window onto the relational aspects of perversion. We can see this as a *danse macabre* duet, a dance of death between a mother who cannot tolerate allowing her daughter to live freely and autonomously, and a daughter who has accepted this perverse contract with her mother in which she essentially says, "I will be your puppet/pianist slave and deny my separateness, existing within the twisted twilight of your control of reality, if you will assure me of half-life, a false dilettantist corruption of true and enlivening creativity, but reassuring me that I am your protégé, the finest pianist of Schuman and Schubert and the best teacher in Vienna." In this way, the film illustrates the relational notion of perversion as "a narrative of how desire and personal agency are translated (perverted) into a compulsory, unwilled, fateful, horrifying, anonymous, impersonal sadomasochistic event." (Stein, 2003)

Erika lives a daylight life of severity and control, but by night, her sexploits take on the desperation of a woman trying to expunge desire altogether while indulging her fascination with male sexuality. We see, for example, that in the unaccounted hours after teaching piano at the Vienna Conservatory, she operates like a demanding, severe dominatrix who lords over her intimidated students. She is distant and humiliates them with her perfectionistic demands. Erika Kohut seethes with transgressive passions, equally driven by her own passions, as well as she is fascinated with the sexual weaknesses and tastes of men (Stoller, 1970).

Dressed in a trench coat with tan kidskin gloves, her costume evokes the proverbial pervert as she passes one of her male students on her way into a local sex shop peepshow booth to sniff ejaculate on discarded tissues left by previous clients; then she voyeuristically spies on a necking couple in a drive-in until the stimulation so overwhelms her, she squats to urinate by their car, revealing a polymorphous perversity heartily fed both by conflicted pre-oedipal as well as oedipal issues. We see the rebellious toddler refusing her mother's control over her potty training, and we see the lusty and curious oedipal child overstimulated by the primal scene. The scene foreshadows a later scene in which a totally deranged Erika mounts her mother in bed seeking sex. When her appalled mother, finally momentarily acknowledging the real incestuous nature and horrifying implications of their perverse duet, calls her off, Erika blurts out, "But I saw your sex!" revealing the extent to which she is unable to protect herself from the boundarilessness of their perversion.

This tortured mother-daughter relationship plays out in two of Professor Kohuüs relationships developed in the film. One is with her most compliant and devoted female student and the student's mother. Like Erika's own mother, Anna Schober (Anna Sigalevitch)'s mother (Susanne Lothar) devotes her entire energy to developing her daughter's musical talent. She speaks for her daughter and appears in many of the daughter's scenes. In a shocking and ambiguous act during a concert, Erika slips out to the concert hall coat room, smashes a crystal glass and places the shards in her student Anna's right coat pocket, knowing it will lacerate and destroy the young pianist's dominant hand.

This shocking act reverberates with her mother's outburst at her in the opening scene of the film when Mother wails: "I should cut your hands off, beating your own mother like that!" As we recoil in horror from the enormity of this act of violence, we are left to question: Is Erika's act an envious assault on a young rival, as when Erika told her mother that Anna has talent for Schubert, mother replied, "Schubert's your department. No one must surpass you!" Or, is the attack a displacement of her rage at her mother's intrusiveness and control? Is it rage at her mother's ambition channeled vicariously through her piano career without regard for her own desires? Or, finally, is Erika simply trying to spare the young pianist the life of enslavement to music (and perhaps her own stage mother) that she feels keeps her "caged in prison 8 hours a day'"?

Perversion Annilihates Creativity and Love

Erika's liaison with Walter Klemmer (Benoit Magimel), the second key relationship where the perverse script is fully elaborated sexually, is introduced at her private piano recital, when she meets her love interest, the hostesses' young nephew, a dashing engineering student and also a talented pianist. Young Klemmer is immediately smitten by her and begins his pursuit, toward which she characteristically turns a cold eye. At the recital reception Erika makes an unsettling remark to him about Schumann's mental breakdown, suggesting she too, could be losing her mind, although we sense that her repressed existence will continue in the same rigid pattern. She asks Klemmer, "Have you read Adorno's Schumann 's Fanatasia in C Minor? He talks of his twilight. It's not when Schumann was bereft of reason. It's just the moment before. A fraction before. It torments him but he clings on, knowing he is losing his mind. It's about his being aware before being completely abandoned." Young Klemmer replies, "You are a good teacher. You talk about things as if they were completely yours." To which she ominously replies, "I can talk about the twilight of the mind. My father died in an insane asylum."

Klemmer, undaunted by her warning, is infatuated with her and can see Erika's beauty despite her plain appearance. Her icy aloofness excites him. He is smart, endowed, musically talented and sophisticated enough to parry with her intellectually. Hardly intimidated by her, the young and brazen pianist auditions successfully at the conservatory so that he can study with her privately. Klemmer's confident charm, musicality, obvious brains, sexuality and ardor are not lost on Erika, but her attraction to him unleashes in her an avalanche of perverse distortions of her own narrative of desire (Wrye 1994).

Haneke explores her torment as it plays out with Klemmer exhaustively but not exploitatively, and we watch as Erika's twisted psyche gives way to the painful deeper truth that music, no matter how inspired, beautiful, romantic, or perfectly rendered, does not truly thrill or give her pleasure. For her, teaching piano and her conditions of loving are both means of maintaining schizoid distance, maintaining control over the internal parental couple (Morgan, 2000)—in this case the dead insane father, and the intrusive suffocating mother.

Obsessively pursuing musical perfectionism to fill up an empty, emotionally starved existence, Erika realizes that since early childhood she has been expected to sacrifice her life for music. Thus we are soon caught up with the real question of whether she can deal with the innocent love Walter offers her as she has so little experience of the mutuality that is key to intimacy. Her only template for relational closeness is a perverse pact in which the other's subjectivity is unknown, unrecognized, foreign and unwanted.

Unlike Ada in Campion's *The Piano*, or Szpilman in Polansky's *The Pianist*, for Erika, playing the piano does not function as a vital transitional object (Milner 1958) that links the pianist to longed for internal objects and provides a wellspring of creativity. While masochistic suffering may represent efforts to "maintain the structural cohesion, temporal stability and positive affective coloration of a precarious or crumbling self-representation." (Stolerow and Lachman (1980) and Ghent, 1990). For Erika Kohut, the piano, like a love object, is more of a fetishistic, dead object used to distance herself from vulnerable feelings, and is more evocative of the inaccessible insanity of her dead father (Alien, 1995; Raphling, 1989; Wrye, 1998).

The three most tortuous and telling scenes in Erika and Klemmer's unfolding affair include the scenes around his qualifying recital for admission to the conservatory. We see him dashingly impress the judges and watch her efforts to repress her own passionate response to him; all that she reveals in terms of feeling during his audition is shown in a barely discernable nervous twitch of her fingers on her thigh. Her public response continues to reveal disdainful diminution of him and all her students.

Then, that night, in a private scene reminiscent of the jarring genital self-mutilation scene in Bergman's Cries and Whispers, Erika returns to her apartment, disrobes and puts on her floral satin robe, closes herself in the bathroom, and in an excruciatingly orchestrated ritual seated on the side of the bathtub, with her legs extended into the empty tub, takes a mirror and a razor blade, and begins cutting her genitals. Clearly Klemmer has cut through her defensive armamentarium and stimulated her. But even more painfully clear, her sexual response to him will be masochistic and horrifyingly self-destructive (Menninger, 1935; Menaker, 1953; Loewenstein, 1957; SchadSomers 1982). As her face reveals exquisite pain and satisfaction, the blood flows into the tub when her mother announces through the closed door, "Dinner is ready!" Erika gathers herself and pregnantly replies, "Coming, Mother!" verbalizing a consummately sadomasochistic abnegation of orgasmic desire in reply to mother's offering of nurture.

The fact that this scene takes place at a bathtub also symbolizes the deflation or lack of the potential warm babymommy and mesensuality of early bathing experiences. Here the basic bodily fluids of maternal-infant caretaking that can signal jouissance—milk, tears, pee and bubblebath—have been replaced by blood—but not the menstrual blood signaling fertility or the blood of childbirth signaling generativity, but a bloody self-mutilated clitoris signing an attack on the sensual body (Mayer, 1985; Holtzman, 1996).

The next scene follows Walter Klemmer's first lessons with Professor Kohut, where he pleads for more contact with her. She refuses, he begs, she finally relents. They meet in the conservatory's public bathroom (once again, the potential intimacy of a bathing room, has become the site for perverse sexuality) where in response to his passionate embrace and entreaties for her love, she draws back, orders him neither to touch her nor to relieve his aching organ through masturbation. Gazing at his engorged organ, she clearly enjoys a voyeur's distanced control of the situation and a sadist's pleasure in humiliating the object (Meyers, 1991). This scene also suggests a reversed reenactment of her own eager childhood exuberance no doubt frustrated repetitively by unsatisfactory and mis-attuned parental responses.

She tells Klemmer she will deliver written instructions to him as to the conditions of their sexual encounters, which turn out to be a detailed letter of instructions for a sadomasochistic sexual encounter aided by assorted S & M apparatus that she keeps hidden under her bed awaiting such an apt and vulnerable partner. Erika Kohut's plan requires profound personal masochistic degradation, and a sadistic control meted out in a dictated duet for both sexual subjects (Biven, 1996) to be carried out within the hearing of her mother, but with the door barred against mother's intrusiveness, using their sounds to execute revenge against her mother.

Young lovesick Walter, who is not really into sadomasochism, allows himself initially to be enlisted out of yearning and curiosity, or perhaps because he hopes she will yield to him more authentically at the end of the scenario. Imagining he has met hidden wildness, he eventually realizes it is madness. In naming it as such and refusing to play, he gains the upper hand, thus utterly humiliating her. From there the film traces Erika Kohut's tortured descent into true madness and final suicide at the Vienna Conservatory during a concert of Schumann, thus attacking her internal object and ending the protracted battle between he who briefly loved without restraint and she who was compelled to make of love a restraint.

In her suicide we see the culmination of a pre-psychotic personality that had used the perversion as a means to contain and protect herself from psychotic disintegration. Once Klemmer refuses to participate in her perverse scripts, and she sees him in the concert hall, returning to "normalcy" by dating an attractive young music student his own age, Erika Kohut loses her fragile defense against psychic fragmentation and symbolically stabs herself to death in the breast in the foyer of the Vienna concert hall, killing off her mother's ambitions, choosing death over life, and giving in to the full blown psychosis of her father and her musical hero, Schumann that she had warned of earlier.

REFERENCES

Allen, R. (1995). "The transitional object, fetishism, and The Piano." Issues in Psychoanal. Psychol. [17] (2): 185-201.

Balter, L. (1969). "The mother as source of power: a psychoanalytic study of three Greek myths." Psychoanal. Quart. 38: 217-274.

Biven, B. M. & Daldin, H. (1996). "Female perversions: the lost continent." Psychoanal. Psychoth. in Africa 4(1): 1-18.

Ceccoli, V. (2003). IIARPP Online Colloquium Series # 2 March 2003. "What Happens When Love Lasts? An Exploration of Intimacy and Erotic Life " Internet.

Elise, D. (1998). "The absence of the paternal penis." J. Amer. Psychoanal. Assn. 46: 413-442.

Ghent, E. (1990). "Masochism as a perversion of surrender." Contemp. Psychoanal. 26: 108-136.

Harris, A. (1993). Envy and excitement masquerades as empowerment: the hidden dilemmas in women's ambition. LA Child Guidance

Center's Conference on Women and Ambition, Sept. 1993, U.C.L.A.

Holtzman, D. K., N. M. (1996). "Nevermore: the hymen and the loss of virginity." J: Amer. Psychoanal. Assn. 44(Spring): 303-332.

Kaplan, L. (1991). Women masquerading as women. Perversions and near-perversions in clinical practice: new psychoanalytic perspectives. G. F. W. Myers. New Haven, Yale Univ. Press: 127-152.

Loewenstein, R. M. (1957(?)). "A contribution to the psychoanalytic theory of masochism." J. Amer. Psychoanal. Assn. Monograph: 197-234.

Mayer, E. L. (1985). "'Everybody must be just like me': observations on female castration anxiety." International Journal of Psycho-Analysis, 66: 331-347.

Menaker, E. (1953). "Masochism--A defense reaction of the ego." Psychoanal. Quart. 22: 205-221.

Menninger, K. A. (1935). "A psychoanalytic study of the significance of self-mutilations." Psychoanal. Quart. 4: 408-466.

Meyers, H. (Nov. 10, 1991). Perversions and everyday life. Sixteenth Annual Scientific Conference of Washington Square Institute, New York, Issues in Ego Psychology.

Milner, M. (1958) Psychoanalysis and art. In: Psychoanalysis and Contemporary Thought ed. J. D. Sutherland. London: Hogarth 1959.

Morgan, M. F. J. (2000). "From fear of intimacy to perversion: A clinical analysis of the film Sex, Lies and Videotape." Brit, Jour. of Psychoth. 17(1): 85-94.

Raphling, D. L. (1989). "Fetishism in a woman." J. Amer. Psychoanal. Assn. 37(2): 465491.

Schad-Somers, S. P. (1982). Sadomasochism: Etiology and Treatment. New York, Human Sciences Press, Inc.

Stein, R. (2003) "Why perversion?" Paper for the International Association of Relational Psychoanalysis and Psychotherapy (IARPP) Online Colloquium, Nov 2003.

Stoller, R. J. (1970). "Pornography and perversion." Archives of General Psychiatry. 22: 490-499.

Stolorow R. D. & Lachman, F. M. (1980) Psychoanalysis of Developmental Arrests. New York: International Universities Press.

Wrye, H. (1996). "Dead babies and the birth of desire: maternal erotic transferences and countertransferences." Jour. of the Amer. Acad. of Psychoanal. 24(1): 75-94.

Wrye, H. K. (1993). "Hello the Hollow: Deadspace or Playspace?" Psych Rev 80(1 (Spring)): 101-122.

Wrye, H. K. (1998). "Tuning a clinical ear to the ambiguous chords of Jane Campion's The Piano." Psych. Inq. 18(2): 168-182.

Wrye, H. K. and J. K. Welles (1994). The Narration of Desire: Erotic Transference and Countertransference. Hillsdale, N.J., The Analytic Press.

CHAPTER NINE ❧

Damage
Directed by Louis Malle (1992)

The Vanishing
Directed by George Sluizer (1988)

Father of the Bride
Directed by Vincente Minnelli (1950); Directed by Charles Shyer (1991)

Fathers Facing Their Daughters' Emerging Sexuality: The Return of the Oedipal Complex

In this study I take a close look at an important phase of human development that is central in Freud's theory. This phase has to do with identification with one parent and competition with the other parent. This phase is called the oedipal phase, based on the play *Oedipes Rex* by Sophocles, in Greek mythology. The theme of the play delves into a boy's passionate love of his mother and desire to marry her and eliminate his father, his rival, so that he can become her one and only love.

I propose that parents revisit their own oedipal passions and conflicts parallel to their children's passages through their oedipal phases. The child's oedipal behavior stirs up in the parent old attachment and separation issues as well as old desires and competitions. This both tests the parent's old solutions and offers the chance of new ones. In my view the parent not only is reacting to the child but is also experiencing the destabilization of his own intrapsychic structures.

Such destabilizing, which occurs in any important period of psychological transition or development, is both promising and potentially dangerous; it opens up the possibility of more mature and more adaptive resolutions of revisited conflicts, but also poses the danger of cracking a brittle or rigid adjustment, prompting a return to more primitive ways of coping. The resulting inner turmoil may produce disruptive thoughts, affects, and sometimes behavior, ranging from temporary benign regression to severe decompensation.

It goes without saying that oedipal revisitations occur in both parents in conjunction with the oedipal stages of children of both sexes, but I focus here on paternal reactions to, and enactments with, daughters. It may be argued that not all men experience such a crisis, although my belief is that most fathers do. This chapter illustrates the way it can appear in a number of different men. Awareness of this possibility helps fathers control their own inappropriate sexual impulses. It also deepens clinical work with men in fathering their daughters.

In the face of their daughter's age-appropriate psychosexual development, some fathers remain both loving and respectful. Others, however, become disturbed, sometimes extremely so. When a man's own oedipal psychology is fragile, the emerging bodily and psychological sexuality of a daughter may trigger highly uncharacteristic reactions, ranging from subtly seductive or punitive behavior to rejection, abandonment, or sexual or violent outbursts.

Periods of intense oedipal feelings can trigger destabilization of internal psychic balance and prior solutions, not only in children, but in their parents as well. Whenever there is such destabilization, old longings reassert themselves, with consequent changes in familiar ways of thinking, feeling, and behaving. A child's oedipal behavior stirs up in the parent old attachment and separation issues as well as old desires and competitions in what may be called the first parental oedipal revisitation. This arousal both tests the parent's old solutions and offers the chance of new ones. The resulting inner turmoil may produce disruptive thoughts, affects, and sometimes behavior.

Psychoanalysis recognizes that being a parent affords many opportunities to regress and potentially rework past and present intrapsychic issues.

Fatherhood, therefore, has been seen as a developmental phase that can profitably be studied in the context of a man's reactions to the development of his children. In the past twenty years or so, we have seen an emphasis on preoedipal issues, often at the expense of oedipal ones. In this study, I want to return to oedipal issues and related aspects of fathers' reactions to their daughters' maturation. I will focus on the father's revisiting of his own unresolved oedipal issues, first in conjunction with his daughter's early childhood oedipal passions and conflicts, and again in conjunction with her adolescent oedipal manifestations. I understand these revisitations to be not only an interpersonal reaction but also an intrapsychic reactivation of the father's own past oedipal experiences. This revisitation offers the father the opportunity to resolve his earlier unresolved issues with or without intervention.

I became interested in this phenomenon during a study of movies, but I soon found that it illuminated my clinical work, with both men and women. In this paper I illustrate some paternal oedipal crises with examples drawn from clinical practice, literature, and film[3]
and discuss some of their developmental contexts and implications.

For example, a patient of mine spoke of admiring his six-year-old daughter's beautiful body while bathing her. He felt sad that she would grow and change and wanted to preserve her image with a photograph. He worried about this thought, recalling a news item about Sally Mann, a photographer,

---

[3] I do not use films as psycho-biographies or to analyze the unconscious of their makers. Rather, I consider them data (Katz and Richards, 1995) that, like clinical data, may be studied in terms of dialogue, events, affect, and behavior, all in the context of the ongoing life situation and historical data available. The advantage of using film in this way is that, since there are no problems with confidentiality, the most intimate details may be presented and discussed. In addition, movies, unlike clinical situations, allow many observers access to the same material. As Freud said about dreams, movies are ideal subjects for analysis in that they use context, condensation, repetition, and visual imagery to convey meaning. Freud himself used literature both to formulate and to illustrate his theories (Freud, 1907, 1913, 1919). Cynthia Ozick (1995) has said that photographs are "a stimulus to the most deliberate attentiveness: time held motionless in a vise of profound concentration, so that every inch of the seized moment can be examined," and this applies to moving pictures as well. Of course movies do not prove anything by themselves. The clinical process provides the only setting in which to test or validate any clinical hypothesis, including those derived from movies. But movies, like literature and life, are an endless source of valuable and test-worthy ideas.

who had taken nude pictures of her children and was then charged with exploiting them sexually. He sensed that taking photographs of a six-year-old in the bath was indeed a sexual overture. This man and his wife had not had sex for several years, and she repeatedly rejected his sexual advances. He became involved with a married woman who offered him the blissful intimacy he dreamed of and craved. This relationship assuaged his deep disappointment in a marriage that was a second edition of his relationship with an adoring but often unavailable mother. In analysis he learned that he needed the extramarital relationship in part to protect himself from acting out inappropriately with his beautiful daughter.

J, a woman in analysis (whose case is described in more detail below), remembered one of her father's Sunday visits during a yearlong marital separation initiated by her mother when J was about five. She told her father of her love for him as well as her anger at him for leaving her. He responded to this passionate declaration by spanking her, something he had never done before and never did again.

Another patient recalled her father's rage when he learned how much she (at fourteen) loved her best girlfriend. He jumped on top of her, pinned her to the floor, and called her a lesbian and a whore.

Developmental Background and Review of the Literature

Since Freud first proposed the concept of the Oedipus complex, it has been elaborated by many contributors to include the psychosexual interactions that occur between parent and child, as well as the intrapsychic fantasies of the child. Freud himself, in "A Child is Being Beaten" (1919), asserted that "The affections of the little girl are fixed on the father *who has probably done all he could to win the little girl*" (p.186; emphasis added).

When a child moves during the first oedipal phase (of early childhood) from a dyadic involvement with each parent toward a triadic one with both at once, the characteristic tensions of passionate love, angry competition, and the need for individuation away from preoedipal merger reach an intense crisis. For each daughter going through this crisis there is also a father who in his own childhood had to make the corresponding effort to identify with his own father and to give up his mother as a potential and exclusively possessed sexual partner. However he managed (or did not manage) these issues, they remain unconsciously present throughout his life. Their repression lightens periodically under certain circumstances. Psychoanalysis is notoriously one of these circumstances (Loewald, 1980). The ordinary course of development provides others.

One such is adolescence, which Blos (1985) defines by two psychosocial events: a loosening of intrapsychic structures that allows oedipal conflicts to recur in the new physical and social context of sexual maturity and desire, and a second stage of separation and individuation. This temporary loosening, when well negotiated, allows adolescent children to reassess their parents as primary love objects and as authorities and thus to develop the psychological independence to go their own ways.

In its content (love, aggression, and separation), the adolescent oedipal crisis resembles the first oedipal period, but it differs sharply in that the new physical maturity of the child raises sexual concerns and possibilities for both adolescent and parent that were not there in early childhood. Also, impending adulthood demands much more decisive separation.

Benedek (1970) correctly asserted that we know more about parents' effects on their children's oedipal development than we do about how they are affected by it. In working to delineate how parents' handling of their own libidinal impulses influences the eventual structure of the child's superego, she suggested that a converse relationship may also exist. For instance, when a child does not resolve the first oedipal crisis adequately, the second crisis may be more turbulent and may therefore create more turmoil in the parent. As the derivatives of the Oedipus complex accumulate over time, keeping them all repressed comes to demand more and more energy. Defenses that were adequate before may break down in adulthood—for instance, under the added burden of the sexual maturation and marriages of children. "Thus the pathologic consequences ... of the oedipal phase (aiming at sexual repression) become manifest often in the middle or old age of parents" (p. 188).

The oedipal crisis may have more benign consequences as well. A colleague told me a story that poignantly illustrates the lifelong vitality of oedipal preoccupations. When her father was almost ninety, still mentally alert, he moved into her home. On the first night of this new arrangement he got briefly confused and asked her worriedly, referring to the son-in-law he adored, "Does Henry know about us?"

Loewald (1980) considered the reactivation of oedipal struggles in adolescence to be normal and expectable, not a pathological solution of the original oedipal problem. He believed that smaller phases of disorganization and reorganization recur throughout life and that, when this happens, previously established psychic structures become plastic once more. I suggest that parenthood is one of these phases, virtually forcing parents to reexperience developmental issues in parallel with their children. Issues that were not adaptively resolved in the parents' own youth, therefore, are potentially disruptive once again during the corresponding stages of parenthood; as is true of other stresses, the more brittle or fragile the parent's psychic structure, the greater the disruptive potential.

Anthony (1970a) sums up this phenomenon: "The oedipal wishes of the parent are often reactivated by the oedipal manifestations in the child." The child's oedipal behavior stirs up old attachment and separation issues in the parent, as well as old desires and competitions. This tests the parent's old solutions and offers the chance of new ones. The parent's oedipal and preoedipal issues are awakened and revisited once more in response to the child's second oedipal phase. As his daughter matures into adolescence, a father has to deal not only with the oedipal issues that her childhood oedipal phase reopened but with the new fact of her physical maturity as well. This gives the child's sexuality an immediacy that was not there the first time around. Anthony (1970b) adds that the stress upon parents at this time is increased by the fact that "the very individual towards whom the parent was able to show overt signs of love during childhood has become a sexually stimulating and taboo object."

For example, Anna O's father somehow managed to let her know that he visited prostitutes (Freud, 1893). This was a seduction in that it invited her to imagine his sexual activities.[4] Anna O's love and sexual feelings for her father are well documented, but one wonders how his oedipal fantasies and

---

[4] Some fathers confide in their daughters about difficult relationships with their wives. This too is a seduction, inviting the daughter to fantasize that she could be a better partner to him (Freud, 1893).

wishes dovetailed with hers, making it harder for him to contain an impassioned situation and contributing to her becoming so overwhelmed and traumatized. Britton, (1999) has enlarged upon this, indicating that Anna's father did not establish the boundaries needed to protect his daughter (and himself) from certain incestuous gratifications; yet at the same time he was harsh and prudish in his criticisms of her lively sexuality.

Anna's symptoms appear to have had components of both fantasy and seduction. But more important to my argument here is what she released in her physician, Josef Breuer. Anna's oedipal passions evoked such a response in him that he considered leaving his wife for her. He then fled from Anna in terror of what he was tempted to do, impregnated his wife (Britton, 1999), and handed Anna's case over to Freud and to history. This seems to me an enactment (not only by her, but by her therapist as well) of her father's erotic entrancement with her when she was an adolescent, and it clearly exemplifies the kind of responsive turmoil I am describing here.

An analysand of mine remembers taking a shower with her father when she was five, at which time he granted her request to touch his penis, after telling her to ask her mother if it was okay. When she reached adolescence, he reminded her of this incident and told her that he had done it to satisfy her curiosity, so that she would be able to control herself with boys. He was at the same time oppressively prudish and very seductive with her, and before she left for college, he told her that "boys have a biological problem—once they get excited, they have no control." She eventually came to understand that he was at once warning her against himself and keeping her away from other men, demanding that she remain asexual so that he could have her all to himself, his own permanently loving little girl.

These two examples illustrate a secondary but important point: that a father's vulnerability to destructive oedipal enactments is influenced by his relationship with his own sexual partner, which may serve as either a protective force or as one that impels him into further acting out. This father often confided in his daughter, and when his wife withdrew in tears to her bedroom after they had a fight, he would ask the child to reach out to her, to help him reestablish his connection with her. The more stable Breuer, however, Anna's father-in-transference and in countertransference, returned to his wife to give her a baby—once more affirming his prowess as a man with an adult woman, and as a father.

Uncontrolled seductive behavior and emotional preoccupation with a daughter are possible clues that a father's equilibrium has been upset by his proximity to his child's passions. Severely restrained emotions and constricted behavior may be equally indicative. For example, one analytic patient with a very passionate and artistic nature recently began to grieve never having had the loving gaze or touch of her father. She never remembered being cherished, cuddled, or consoled by him when she was sad or ill. Despite his emotional and physical distance she revered him as the most important and valued member of the family. She feared that her longings and rage would hurt him, and so she desperately strove to control herself. His own harsh constraints further forestalled any lively interaction between them, and I assume that he thereby rigidly defended himself against any desires or aggressions that might have been aroused by his daughter's oedipal turmoil.

These are extreme parental defenses, and they restrict opportunities for growth-enhancing engagement in both father and daughter. In more fortunate cases, says Anthony (1970a), "[appropriate] parental defenses" arise in response to the child's emerging sexuality, and these permit new opportunities for growth-enhancing engagement. Such appropriate parental defenses, when effective, allow the parent to handle the anxiety provoked by his own reactivated incestuous fantasies.

Colarusso (1990, pp. 179-194) has emphasized that the onset of puberty in a child provokes further individuation in the parent, who must rework rekindled infantile themes while learning to accept the adolescent's mature body and its implications for both of their futures. The parent must gradually replace his internal representation of an immature and dependent child with that of a physically and sexually mature person—one who is preparing to replace the parents as the most significant persons in his or her life. Thus the parents' responses to the child's sexual maturation are not only a reaction to the child, but also a result of the adults' own continuing psychological development.

Furthermore, the onset of puberty in their children often coincides with a separate developmental passage in parents' own lives, which includes the fact of their aging and often the loss of their own parents: the so-called "midlife crisis." This is another reason that the onset of puberty in children may be a time of extreme stress for parents—and for children too, as an adolescent patient pointed out when she said that the coincidence of her puberty and her mother's menopause was "absolutely the worst!" Child and parent at the same time face the unbalancing of their previous inner and outer adjustments. And while parents struggle to parent the mercurial adolescent appropriately, they must at the same time refocus their own quests for fulfillment in love and work as the child moves away.

Erikson (1950) called this crossroads the phase of generativity vs. stagnation. Generativity is primarily an interest in establishing and guiding the next generation. When the sublimation of instinctual needs does not occur or cannot be maintained under stress, "a regression from generativity to an obsessive need for pseudo-intimacy, punctuated by moments of mutual repulsion, takes place, often with a pervading sense (and objective evidence) of individual stagnation and interpersonal impoverishment" (p. 231). I take this to mean that people who have not sufficiently mastered the anxieties of separation and intimacy and who do not have a reliable capacity to tolerate ambivalence may lack the ability to subsume their own desires in the interest of another's good. In these cases the demands of parenting may provoke regressions in which the desires reassert themselves and even take control, or else are defensively and rigidly sealed over.

Ferenczi (1933) addressed this situation directly. He was one of the first psychoanalysts to speak with compassion about the difference between the tender love of the child for the father, and some fathers' passionate pathological response, mistaking it for a sign of the child's readiness and capacity actually to engage in sexual relations. That is, he distinguished sharply between the expression and intention of love in the child's world and in the world of the mature adult. (It would appear that Breuer understood this distinction very well intuitively, and so was able to keep himself from actual sexual enactment with Anna O. Still, his feelings disturbed him profoundly. An intellectual understanding of what is going on is not always enough to keep the waters calm, as the father mentioned above who wanted to photograph his daughter discovered.)

Examples from Films

One of the values of literature and film is that they portray the human condition in a very dramatic fashion, thus helping to call attention to universal human predicaments whose more ordinary manifestations are not always noticed in everyday life. Although fortunately we do not usually see such extreme examples in the real world or in clinical practice, nevertheless we are expanded and enriched when an artist's interest in a psychological situation (sometimes exaggerated by artistic necessity) elicits and informs our own. Therefore, I offer here two portrayals from films of fathers who decompensated catastrophically under the stress of their daughters' maturation. Three clinical examples demonstrate more moderate decompensations, and a final film shows a contrasting healthy adjustment to this phase.

As I understand them, the films *Damage* and *The Vanishing* (the original Dutch version) focus on the breakdown of apparently normal but precariously compensated fathers in the face of an adolescent daughter's emerging sexuality. These fathers are rigidly controlled, obsessive-compulsive men who are accomplished and successful in their careers but incapable of flexible relationships with other people and are engaged in distant and libidinally dead marriages.

In Louis Malle's *Damage*, the father, Stephen (played by Jeremy Irons), is dismayed to note the blossoming of his fourteen-year-old daughter, Sally (played by Gemma Clarke). He becomes sexually obsessed with his son's fiancée. There are obviously father-son oedipal issues at work here as well, but I believe that in this film the daughter's developing sexuality and separation have the more insidious effect on the father's oedipal and preoedipal desires. Of course, the combination of these stresses makes the situation all the more difficult for the father. His need for union with the surrogate daughter takes him over completely, and his uncontrollable affair with her eventually leads to tragedy.

In *The Vanishing*, Raymond (portrayed by Bernard-Pierre Donnadieu), the father, is suddenly confronted with the full impact of his seductive, idealizing fourteen-year-old daughter, and it unhinges him. He becomes obsessed with devising and carrying out a plan to entice a young woman who looks like his daughter into his car. But instead of enjoying sex with her, he chloroforms her and buries her alive. After committing this perfect crime, he goes back to living his life with his family as before.[5]

The fathers in both of these movies are driven to bizarre and uncharacteristic action by the feelings stirred up by their enticing adolescent daughters and the concomitant fear of eventual abandonment by the daughters. Stephen acts out his need for perfect fusion with an adoring daughter substitute. Unbalanced by his daughter's emerging sexuality and her movement away from him toward a boyfriend, he becomes enthralled with a woman who seems enraptured with him and desperate to have him, and who promises never to leave him even if she marries another, in this case his son.

Raymond, overwhelmed by his daughter's love and by her exciting idealization of him, finds a psychotic solution to his sexual arousal and conflict. He buries his desires with the other young woman and so saves his own daughter from his violence and sexuality. As Ferenczi (1933) cautioned: "Parents and adults, in the same way as we analysts, ought to learn to be constantly aware that behind the submissiveness or even the adoration, just as behind the transference love, of our children, patients and pupils, there lies hidden an ardent desire to get rid of this oppressive love" (p. 164). The image of the praying mantis—a species in which the female often bites off the head of her mate after copulation—at the beginning and end of *The Vanishing* reminds us ominously of the danger of desire for men like Raymond, who are still trapped in primitive forms of loving.

Examples from Clinical Practice

These examples from my practice, at a lesser pitch of intensity, illustrate the same issues.

One father was sufficiently aware of his difficulty managing his own and his daughter's passions that he came into treatment for that reason. Mr. R had custody of his fourteen-year-old, who had campaigned for this

---

[5] George Sluizer, the director, told me that he tested his daughter for the role of the abducted girl but decided not to cast her in the part after concluding that she had more talent as a director than as an actress. Nevertheless, he said, she was "an inspiration for the role of Saskia," and he chose actress Johanna ter Steege for the role "not mainly, but also because she had a physical resemblance to my daughter."

arrangement. She idolized her father and hated her mother. He thrived on her adulation but also feared it. He came to therapy because he was disturbed by the sudden and intense rages that erupt against her. And when she was angry at him, he felt devastated, and would suggest to her that she would be happier living with her mother. He was sexually inappropriate and invasive with his daughter, taking her to near-pornographic movies and sharing too much information about his girlfriends. As she became more able to separate from him, with the help of her own therapist, and to establish friendships with her peers, he began to act out with young women close to her age, demonstrating his continuing difficulty in managing his sexual and aggressive passions.

Mr. R was very attached to his mother and alienated from his father. Manifestly conciliatory and compliant with men, he was aware of feeling very competitive and secretly disdainful of them. He also felt superior to his estranged wife. His attachment to his mother, whom he greatly admired, and his contempt of his father and his wife contributed to the revisited oedipal struggles which were eventually acted out with his daughter.

A more extensive example concerns Mr. P, who had been reluctant to have a child because he was furious at his own father's abuse when he was a child and fearful that he would repeat it with his own child. When he and his wife decided to adopt, he would consider only a daughter, lest a son would set him up to repeat what his father had done to him. (Even so, aggressive impulses toward little boys came to the fore in a frightening way when he had to struggle to keep himself from grabbing and overpowering some rowdy boys who were playing with his daughter.) Years of previous analytic work enabled him to make the decision to adopt and become a loving father to his daughter. In this example, I will focus on his analytic work at the time of his daughter's first oedipal phase (between ages three and seven).

Mr. P was an accomplished professional in a field in which both parents had also excelled. As a child he longed for the love and attention of his mother, whom he saw as fragile and oppressed by her husband. He saw his father as a bully and tyrant who responded to his son's every attempt at defiance or disobedience with painful and humiliating beatings. We came to understand, however, that these beatings were unconsciously orchestrated by the son; they were a masochistic and predictable way of getting his father's attention and thereby controlling him and vindicating himself for his murderous rage at his father and his fantasies of destroying him.

Mr. P's narcissistic mother both overstimulated and neglected him. She also colluded with his oedipal desires. At bedtime he would keep himself awake for hours with fantasies of heroic conquests, waiting for the sound of her footsteps at the top of the stairs; when he called her, she would come and gratify his request for yet another kiss despite the father's prohibition.[6] Mr. P's father colluded by not stopping this peculiar manifestation of the oedipal struggle. Mr. P now has sleeping problems.

As an adult, he has identified with his parents in his choice of profession. But his identification with his father has not been successful, in that he feels blocked in his research and unable to participate in necessary competitive professional efforts.

Mr. P's marriage to a lively, nurturing woman allowed him to be the center of attention and to receive the love that had been missing in his childhood. When she "failed" him, he became rageful and depressed. She would either cater to him or reject him, leaving him feeling either guilty, or enraged and forsaken. Mr. P believed that having frequent sex with his wife would enable him to feel good; at first his wife gratified this wish, knowing that his depression would lift, and he would become easier to live with. But as she became more separate from him as a result of her own analytic work, she catered to him less in this way, leaving him ashamed that he felt so unmanly and needy.

The decision to adopt a child, although initiated by his wife, provided pleasure and joy in Mr. P's life, but as his daughter now traversed her first oedipal passage, he experienced an upsurge of his own issues. He found her enchanting and enjoyed playing with her, making her giggle with delight, touching her soft body, looking at her, making up stories for her, and drawing with her. He was aware that he was revisiting his childhood and re-finding something that was lost or absent at that time. But he was also always aware that he is her father. Though at times Mr. P finds it difficult to maintain appropriate boundaries, when he feels aroused, hurt, or enraged

---

[6] Proust, who had also waited long hours for his mother's kiss, eventually became one of his favorite authors.

he works very hard at keeping himself from acting out inappropriately with the child. He is gaining both pleasure from and mastery over his infantile urges to merge in connection with her. Through playful regressions with his daughter and through his transference regression with me, he is now reworking his oedipal and preoedipal desires and conflicts.

About a year and a half ago, some overt acting out of the oedipal relationship appeared between this father and his daughter. At that time, when the child (age five and a half) woke in the middle of the night and couldn't fall back to sleep easily, she would go into her father's bedroom and sleep on a mattress next to his bed. (At Mrs. P's suggestion, he and his wife did not share a room at that time because of her long-standing sleeping difficulties.) He did not allow his daughter in his bed, both out of his awareness that this would harm her and out of fear that he himself would become aroused. However, he enjoyed these special midnight trysts with his daughter (reminiscent of his waited-for late-night kisses with his mother).

Clearly, Mr. P's relationship with his wife is a factor in the balance of his relationship with his daughter.[7] When his wife withholds the indulgence and loving devotion he yearns for, it is hard for him to express his anger and disappointment directly; he either resists passively or cooperates reluctantly. He avoids taking a stance in strong and firm opposition to her for fear of turning into the bully his father was. These fears are less evident in his relationship with his daughter. He clearly feels more secure in loving his small daughter and even fighting with her.

However, Mr. P is learning and growing from the experience with the child, as is she. Within a year, the mattress in Mr. P's bedroom had been removed, and she could put herself back to sleep in her own room when she woke up. At the same time, and not coincidentally, Mr. P's sexual relationship with his wife had become more lively and pleasurable, and he was increasingly considerate of and responsive to her. But oedipal feelings never lose their

---

[7] I have found it to be generally true that the capacity to form a good relationship with an adult woman is a prognostic criterion for the capacity to handle a daughter's development. A good marital relationship is both a mark of having resolved original oedipal conflicts reasonably well and an outlet for freshly aroused passions. It is also a source of support when oedipal conflicts are revisited in parenthood.

touch of danger. When Mrs. P went away for a two-day trip, the child couldn't stop giggling. I asked Mr. P what he thought that meant, and he said: "I think it was defensive—that she misses her mother." I said "Really?" "Well," he then said, "maybe she was excited about being alone with me." Mr. P's initial denial of his daughter's glee at her exclusive access to him betrayed his own longing to be the one and only—to his daughter, his wife, his mother, and perhaps his father.

A few months after this, Mr. P's father died, and his mother turned to him for the kind of professional support her husband had given her. Her preference for her son's more patient manner both pleased and disturbed Mr. P. The too real gratification of his oedipal fantasies resulted in sexual difficulties with his wife. He saw her as "too big." His daughter's size felt more comfortable to him. After several months of analysis, this symptom subsided.

The intergenerational aspects of the oedipal constellation came up dramatically in a dream after his father's death, when intense oedipal and preoedipal longings for me were emerging in the transference. The day residue was his daughter's telling him of a dream in which she had to choose between having mommy and daddy die while she herself lived, or having mommy live while she and daddy died. She chose the latter. Mr. P had seen this as a reversal and an oedipal dream. That night he had an oedipal dream of his own, in which he and his mother were naked, and his father was fully clothed. He saw this as a reversal of a primal scene he had witnessed in childhood, in which his parents were naked, and he was clothed. The rest of the content of this complex dream illustrated both his own oedipal conflicts and his parents' seductive collusion in them. He summed up his associations by saying: "I need my father, and I want to replace him."

He then thought of the movie *Burnt by the Sun*, (directed by Nikita Mikhalkov). which portrays a powerful and beautiful oedipal relationship between a father and his six-year-old daughter (played by the director and his own daughter; see note 3). He empowers and loves her in an appropriate way, clearly not substituting her for his wife, with whom he has an intimate, sensual relationship. But what Mr. P could not forget in this movie was the horrifying scene at the very end: the father, a previously esteemed general in the Communist party, is taken prisoner by the Stalinists and blinded by one of his erstwhile subordinates. Mr. P's association to this is castrating the father.

My third clinical example, mentioned briefly above, concerns the father of an analytic patient, J, who was trying to come to terms with some uncharacteristic and disturbing behavior of her father, Mr. D, so that she could begin to forgive him.

Mr. D's mother had loved her sons more than her daughters, but she paid less attention to Mr. D than to her husband or her older son, often leaving him feeling less valuable than his father and brother. He felt that his father also favored the first-born son. In spite of documented acts of heroism as he got older and evidence of a strong and generous nature, he never resolved the fear that he was inferior to his older brother and his brilliant father, and he suffered from the conviction that his brother alone had his father's true regard. Therefore Mr. D's own oedipal development seems to have been based on a difficult disjunction. His mother's belief that manhood was all-important, combined with his father's apparent reluctance to confirm Mr. D's possession of it, left his feeling insecure and vulnerable.

He tended to overcompensate for this sense of inferiority by trying hard to please, but he remained very vulnerable to small slights. Thus, although he enjoyed women—presumably thanks to his comfort in his mother's love, however flawed—he still felt, on a fundamental level, profoundly insecure as a man. The complex constellation of his own first and second oedipal phases—his mother's overvaluation of males along with his father's "withholding" of full recognition of Mr. D's manhood—was the background of his relationship with his wife and children, and it remained an undertow in his experience of his own daughter's oedipal phases.

Mr. D also felt frustrated and thwarted in his attempts to possess the second edition of the object of desire—his wife. He had married a woman whom he loved deeply and who represented his romantic dream. Still, this love was often ridden with conflict and tension. Both of them were fragile and easily hurt, and they enacted with each other their futile longings for a mother's loving acceptance and attention. Both experienced disappointment and hurt when such acceptance was not forthcoming. Mr. D felt devalued by his wife when, for instance, she criticized him for not measuring up to her own (idealized) father. And he could not tolerate her depressed or angry withdrawals from him; he experienced these as a humiliation and a loss and reacted with anger.

J believed that her father loved and enjoyed his children. Still, from time to time he behaved uncharacteristically. His inner turmoil, usually well contained, was reactivated periodically during his daughter's oedipal phases. When her sexuality was especially evident his behavior was sometimes very disturbing—so much so that when she came into analysis, she needed to deny her love for her father and his importance to her.

Her denial had roots in an incident that occurred when J was about five, and Mr. and Mrs. D had (temporarily) separated. J had passionately told her father how much she loved him and how angry she was at him for leaving her. Mr. D responded to this declaration by spanking her for the only time in her life. This unique rageful reaction appeared to be a defense against the sexual feelings J had aroused at a time of rejection by his wife, and possibly a reaction to the hurt and anger she had expressed.

When J turned fourteen, her father again had unpredictable outbursts of fury at her. She was now a feisty teenager with a boyfriend and, as he saw it, no longer the loving, adoring daughter he had enjoyed in the past; he saw her as rebellious and defiant. In the past they had negotiated disagreements fairly easily, but now he would sometimes go for weeks without speaking to her. This again was highly extreme and unusual behavior. (Furthermore, when things were better between them, Mrs. D tended to become very jealous of his attentions to J and would accuse him of having affairs; this added yet another level of unsafety to this father's and daughter's enjoyment of each other.)

Mr. D also proved surprisingly resistant when the time came for J to go off to college. He offered her enticements (a car, for instance) to stay home, and when she persisted in her wish to leave, he found it very difficult to let her go. He did finally come to terms with her departure, support her strivings for independence, and return to his old loving self. But early in her transitions, turmoil always seemed to overtake him for a while.

Similarly, when J married, in her early thirties, he was apparently happy with and supportive of this decision. Yet he also told her at that time that for ten years he had been having an affair with a married woman very close to her age.

Mr. R, Mr. P, and Mr. D, although in considerably better shape than the fathers in the films discussed above, displayed some of the same characteristics. They were professionally successful and well established in life. They were basically devoted and caring fathers. Mr. D and Mr. P had stable, although troubled, relationships with their wives; Mr. R was divorcing his wife. All these fathers had unresolved competitive feelings toward other men. They longed for the loving attention of a woman; the adoration of their oedipal daughters fulfilled that desire. Yet when this was withheld or turned elsewhere, they once again felt the pain of oedipal rejection and became enraged, as is especially evident with Mr. D.

Mr. P, in analysis himself, was able to become aware of what he was going through intrapsychically and to avoid acting out these feelings with his daughter; he is still working on his oedipal issues. Mr. D continued to act out his issues in his affairs with young women his daughter's age. Mr. R left therapy before he could have a chance to work out these issues.

A healthy negotiation of parental oedipal revisiting was depicted in both film versions of *Father of the Bride*. This father is a warm, concerned parent and an engaged and loving husband. He possesses the ability to reflect, and to contain disturbing feelings. When he learns that his daughter is engaged, he oscillates between terror and rage, and engages in furious competitive and murderous fantasies against the intruding young man. But however inwardly confused and regressed he feels, he remains outwardly supportive of his daughter. Throughout, he is also intimately connected with his wife as friend and lover—and sometimes as mentor in parenting. This father's ambivalence is clear: He wants his daughter to be happy, so he supports the wedding; but he wants his little girl back, and so he resists it. In the first version of the film, the father has a nightmare the night before the wedding: first he can't move his feet to walk down the aisle, then his clothes start to come off. In the dream he is impotent, castrated, and humiliated. But he later regains his emotional balance enough to realize that: "My daughter— she's my daughter all of her life." Clearly this father is actively working through his developmental crisis. He mourns the loss of his little girl; he forgives her for loving another man; and he accepts her as a separate, sexual woman. He comes to understand that she still loves him, and he becomes able to love her in a new way.

Not all fathers can understand or accept this kind of love. Shakespeare's King Lear could not. When he decides to divide his kingdom as his last and most beloved daughter comes of age, he is enraged by her response to his question about how much she loves him: "I love your majesty according to my bond; nor more nor less.... Haply, when I shall wed, that lord whose hand must take my plight shall carry half my love with him." He cannot grasp the fact that the true love of her father also prepares a girl to love a mate (Tessman, 1989, p. 197).

Discussion

Men are more affected by their daughters' maturation than is generally recognized, and as I have shown, intrapsychic destabilization in the face of this stress is not uncommon.

The pre-oedipal and oedipal periods are bound together by their focus on blissful love-union, although they make different use of this love and the fantasies attached to it. Preoedipal growth builds on the actual experience of dyadic bonding, and oedipal growth on the need to relinquish the fantasy of possession and the ability to recognize and accept that there is a third person involved (or a connection to another that may exclude oneself). Many clinicians feel that relinquishment is not possible without an original "good-enough" experience. When this does not occur, successful resolution of the oedipal situation is very much more difficult.

Furthermore, the very idea of love may become tainted. When reality is too harsh or frustrating, the child may cling to omnipotent magical fantasies rather than developing competent and realistic ways of gaining gratification. The Novicks (1996), for example, think that in mother-child dyads in which disruptions are not repaired by the mother but instead become repetitive and fixed, a sadomasochistic orientation to life takes root early in the baby's infancy. Patterns of connecting through pain rather than pleasure, and through fantasies of omnipotent control, rather than competence or effectance, begin early and become established. (Mr. P is an example of this.) Eventually attempts to control the self and others through pain may feel predictable, reliable, powerful, and safe; trying to connect through love and pleasure-seeking leaves the individual feeling vulnerable and at risk of being abandoned. Thus, the Novicks found that early dyadic failures of this sort lead to a strong attachment to omnipotent fantasies and solutions that then color the oedipal struggles. These may dominate in marriage; later in life an adoring five-year-old daughter, or a maturing adolescent one, may strongly arouse such fantasies and seem to offer a better opportunity to fulfill them than does the complex relationship with a spouse.

As development proceeds, these omnipotent patterns adapt to the new demands of each phase—for drive gratification, self-esteem, attachment, and so forth—and are in turn modified by them, so that the wish to be libidinally attached and to surrender (that is, "to yield and be receptive to another's longings as well as to one's own" [Ghent 1990]) may be perverted into enactments (Katz, 1990) in which omnipotence rather than mutuality is the issue.

Anthony (1993) and Bergmann (1992) stress the critical importance of the environment in the resolution of the Oedipus complex. Mother and father not only are internally represented but are also outwardly interacting persons, both with each other and with the child. Bergmann states: "To reach the oedipal phase as a developmental phase demands a family atmosphere that is reasonably loving toward the child." Searles (1965) stresses the importance of the father's finding a comfortable and appropriate way to experience and express his own attraction and desire for his daughter. He sees this as a crucial factor in the daughter's successful resolution of her oedipal issues, and an enriching and enlivening experience for the father as well. He suggests that this works best in the context of a good marital relationship.

Searles adds that there is a corresponding truth—the importance of the analyst's finding an appropriate way to experience and recognize the attractiveness and desirability of his female analysands. A colleague has told me that when she was an adolescent, she was very unhappy about her father's constrained and distant stance with her. One evening at dinner with her and a classmate, her father, somewhat loosened up by liquor, blurted out: "You know, it's really hard having a daughter. She is my flesh and blood—but she is also a woman!" Uncomfortable with his own feelings and impulses toward her, he had pulled back from her, and this had left her feeling undesirable as a woman and devalued as a person. Realizing that her father did find her attractive helped my colleague feel better about herself.

The capacity to integrate ambivalence is undermined when the parents' hatred in primary object relationships is too strong; there must also be a great deal of love. Winnicott (1971) added to this the importance of a parent's allowing himself to be used by the child as an object of aggression and desire without retaliating in mind. The parent who can psychically survive such behavior furthers the child's development in affect tolerance and in reality testing, and therefore in separation/individuation.

In adverse conditions, though, people do not easily achieve this balance between distance and accessibility, separateness and connectedness, and control of emotions and passionate expression of them. One man's desire for his wife evaporated, so fearful was he of being swept away by the passions excited by a sexually mature woman whom he saw as strong but also critical, rejecting, and even annihilating. The love and attention of his adolescent daughter felt much safer and stirred up intense sexual longing about which he felt guilty and frightened.

For some individuals, it feels necessary to destroy the powerful and exciting other in order to achieve the desired sense of fulfilled infantile omnipotence. Raymond in *The Vanishing* exemplifies this. Anthony adds that some fathers use oppressive methods to try to keep their children under their control and by these means "attempt to recapture the vanishing object" (p. 329). King Lear is an example of such oppressive methods.

According to Meloy (1992), "In a sense, preoedipal personality organization permits, or releases, the acting out of homicidal or violent impulses"—as in the extreme fictional examples of Raymond and Stephen. I would add incestuous impulses as well. Such personality organization may not be chronic, Meloy continues, but instead "an acute state in which a particular disinhibitor, such as extreme stress, … causes regression from a more mature, oedipal level of organization to a preoedipal level of personality."

Mourning is the lasting and healthy alternative to such magical resolutions of dysphoric fantasies and affects (Kavaler-Adler, 1993). The capacity to mourn lost objects and impossible wishes is necessary to the work of resolving the oedipal and separation crises of childhood and adolescence, and therefore it has much to do with an adults' capacity to tolerate oedipal (and other) developmental stresses.

The development of a sense of separateness includes painful awareness of the consequences of one's actions and choices. Once a child recognizes that the loved parent is the same as the hated one, and that the loving parent is the same one who sometimes inflicts pain, she recognizes, too, that injuries to the hated parent are felt as well by the beloved one. The capacity to tolerate ambivalence and the dysphoric affects that go with it and the capacity to forgive both one's parents and oneself for perceived imperfections—ultimately allows the integration on which a solid self is built. It allows the "lost" perfect object to be found again as imperfect, and restored within the internal world, where it can endure, to provide the building blocks of a permanent sense of self. When one knows that reparation can be made, one can own one's own failures and even cruelties. Sadness, regret, remorse, and gratitude are the effects of reparation. The growing capacity of the child to endure them allows the transition away from splitting and toward integrating other and self into individuals who are both good and bad, both loved and hated. Mourning and forgiveness allow the child to repair threatened connections and to maintain within himself ambivalently held images of important others; they therefore allow an increasing openness to others as separate people (Kavaler-Adler, 1993).

The capacity to mourn enables well-integrated adults to use fantasy and symbol to reflect upon and creatively resolve fears and desires, and it frees them from the need for compulsive action. It enables the development of the adaptive capacity to feel without acting and without being trapped. The need for perfection in self and object may lead to action on homicidal and incestuous impulses, or to constrict or shut down threatening feelings. Ibsen's Peer Gynt expresses the difference: "The thought, perhaps the wish to kill, / That I can understand, but really / To do the deed. Ah no, that beats me."

But without the capacity to mourn, these fantasies and expectations are never really recognized as impossible, or ever given up. People who have had trouble mourning the losses of their own first and second oedipal expectations may be unable to maintain their equilibrium in the face of the idealization, anger, or ambivalence of an oedipal child.

Adults who cannot mourn the loss of perfect union, perfect object, or perfect self, or who cannot, however sadly, relinquish impossible wishes, are as susceptible as children when the seeming possibility of blissful fulfillment appears again. And those who cannot tolerate ambivalence sufficiently to be able to reflect upon and contain dysphoric affects are as vulnerable as adolescents to the pressure to act on stressful feelings. For instance, there are men who have never been able to accept the fact that their mothers loved and needed their fathers for something they as children could not supply (Chasseguet-Smirgel, 1978, 1976). They have never been able to accept the end of their dreams of omnipotence and perfection. If they become unbalanced enough, the apparent new chance to realize these dreams may cause such men to blur generational distinctions or lose touch with the realities of parenting. They may then act out, either by seeking their daughters (directly or in displacement) as partners, or by abandoning and rejecting them as sexual, sensual, and assertive beings.

Healthy passage through the parental oedipal and preoedipal revisitations requires that the father be able to give up the dream of perfect union with the daughter—as he has had to give it up already with his mother and his wife—to mourn its loss, and to forgive both himself and her, and to acknowledge the limitations and boundaries that reality imposes upon us all.

Sander (1995) has asked, "What is it that determines the unity of an enduring, coherent sense of identity in one individual, and the disorganization of an 'identity diffusion' in another?" (p. 583). This is a question that can be asked about any of the developmental vicissitudes. In my experience four considerations best assess how well a man is likely to handle the oedipal revivals: 1) his basic character structure and the nature of his intrapsychic adjustment prior to the onset of this life passage; 2) the degree of comfort, intimacy, and gratification that he experiences in his present relationship with his partner; 3) the nature of the other life stresses or transitions that are occurring at the same time—in his other children or his career, for example; and 4) the presence or absence of other important people in his life, such as an esteemed father figure, a mentor, or a psychoanalyst.

Character structure and intrapsychic adjustment are the foundation of all of these, of course. Ultimately it is they that permit or prevent intimate relationships with others, and in so doing determine specifically the sort of marriage a person makes and therefore the amount of support and gratification the marriage provides. They also establish the ability, or lack of it, to connect with other people and use them constructively in nonsexual ways, and they tend to dictate characteristic ways of handling stresses. All four considerations are interconnected. A shaky oedipal resolution predisposes a man to a shaky or unfulfilling marriage; the shaky marriage will make him further vulnerable to decompensation when oedipal fantasies and passions are reawakened.

Conclusion

Many men, regardless of their level of psychic health or pathology, revisit their own oedipal passions and conflicts during a daughter's two primary oedipal phases. I believe that these periods involve the destabilizing of intrapsychic structures, although some argue that they are simply reactions to a daughter at intense periods of her own development.

I have attempted to show that a daughter's development challenges her father's capacity for dealing with the conflicts of love, loss, rage, and desire. Therefore her own struggles with these conflicts and with separation/individuation may be significant determinants of his experience and behavior. The strength of the father's psyche and his capacity to deal with issues of separation, competition, and desire determine whether growth will occur or whether repression or acting out will prevail during these periods when his child's complementary passions unleash once more the impossible dream of perfect exclusive union.

REFERENCES

Anthony, E. J. (1993). Psychoanalysis and environment. In The Course of Life, Vol. 6: Late Adulthood. Eds. George H. Pollock and Stanley I. Greenspan. Madison, Conn.: International Universities Press.

Anthony, E. J. (1970). The Reactions of Parents to Adolescents and to Their Behavior, in Parenthood, Its Psychology and Psychopathology, eds. E. James Anthony and Therese Benedek. Boston: Little, Brown and Co.

Benedek, T. (1970). Parenthood During the Life Cycle, in Parenthood Its Psychology and Psychopathology, eds. E. James Anthony and Therese Benedek. Boston: Little, Brown and Company, 185-206.

Bergmann, M. S. (1992). In the Shadow of Moloch: The Sacrifice of Children and Its Impact on Western Religions. New York: Columbia University Press.

Breuer, J. (1893). Case Histories. Case 1. Fraulein Anna O. S.E. 2:21-48.

Blos, P. (1985). Toward an Altered View of the Male Oedipus Complex: The Role of Adolescence, in Blos, Son and Father: Before and Beyond the Oedipus Complex, N.Y.: The Free Press, 135-173.

Britton, R. (1999). Getting in on the Act: The Hysterical Solution. *Int. J. Psycho-Anal.* 80:1-14.

Chasseguet-Smirgel, J. (1976). Some Thoughts on the Ego Ideal: A Contribution to the Study of the "Illness of Ideality." *Psychoanal. Q.* 45:345-373.

Chasseguet-Smirgel, J. (1974). Perversion, Idealization and Sublimation. *Int. J. Psycho-Anal.* 55, 349.

Colarusso, C. (1990). The Third Individuation: The Effect of Biological Parenthood on Separation-Individuation Processes in *Adulthood. Psychoanal. St. Child* 45. New Haven: Yale University Press.

Erikson, E. H. (1950). Childhood and Society. New York: W. W. Norton & Company.

Ferenczi, S. (1933). Confusion of Tongues, in Final Contributions to the Problems and Methods of Psychoanalysis. Ed. Michael Balint (1955). New York: Brunner/Mazel, 156-167.

Freud, S. (1905). Fragment of an Analysis of a Case of Hysteria. S.E. 7:3-122.

Freud, S. (1907). Delusions and Dreams in Jensen's "Gradiva." S.E. 9:3.

Freud, S. (1910). First Lecture. S.E. 11:9.

Freud, S. (1910). Second Lecture. S.E. 11:21.

Freud, S. (1913). Theme of the Three Caskets. S.E. 12:291.

Freud, S. (1919). A Child is Being Beaten: A Contribution to the Study of the Origin of Sexual Perversions. S.E. 17:177.

Freud, S. (1919). The Uncanny. S.E. 17:219.

Ghent, E. (1990). Masochism, Submission and Surrender: Masochism as a Perversion of Surrender. *Contemp. Psychoanal.*, 26, 108-136.

Jacobson, E. (1964). The Self and the Object World. New York: International Universities Press.

Ibsen, Henrik (1867). "Peer Gynt"

Katz, A. (1990). Paradoxes of Masochism. *Psychoanal. Psychol.* 7:225-242.

Katz, A., & Richards, A. K. (1995). Unpublished discussion.

Kavaler-Adler, S. (1993). The Compulsion to Create. New York: Routledge.

Klein, M. (1940). Mourning and Reparation. London: Hogarth.

Klein, M. (1975). Love, Guilt and Reparation & Other Works, 1921-1945. Delacorte Press/Seymour Lawrence.

Levinson, D. J. (1978). The Seasons of a Man's Life. New York: Ballantine Books, pp. 221-256.

Loewald, H. W. (1980). Comments on Some Instinctual Manifestations of Superego Formation. Papers on Psychoanalysis. New Haven: Yale University Press, pp. 326-341.

Loewald, H. W. (1979). The Waning of the Oedipus Complex. *JAPA.* 27:751-776.

Mahler, M. S., Pine, F., & Bergman, I. (1975). The Psychological Birth of the Human Infant. New York: Basic Books.

Meloy, J. R. (1992). Violent Attachments. Northvale, N.J.: Jason Aronson Inc.

Novick, J., & Novick, K. K. (1996). Fearful Symmetry. Northvale, N.J.: Jason Aronson Inc.

Ozick, C. (1995). More Than Just a Victorian. p. 1 ff. The New York Times Book Review.

Ross, J. M. (1994). What Men Want, Mothers, Fathers, and Manhood. Cambridge, Mass. and London, England: Harvard University Press.

Sander, L. W. (1995). Identity and the Experience of Specificity in a Process of Recognition: Commentary on Seligman and Shanok. *Psychoanal. Dial.*, V 5, 4. 579-593.

Searles, H. F. (1995). Collected Papers on Schizophrenia and Related Subjects. New York: International Universities Press.

Segal, H. (1957). Notes on Symbol Formation. *Int. J. Psycho-Anal.* 38:391-397.

Shakespeare, W. *King Lear.* Act 1, Scene 1. Lines 92 and 93, and 100-102.

Sluizer, G. (2001). Personal Communication.

Tessman, L. H. (1989). Fathers and Daughters, Early Tones, Later Echoes. "Fathers and Their Families" edited by Cath, S. H., Gurwitt, A., and Gunsberg, L., Hillsdale, N.J.: Analytic Press.

Winnicott, D. W. (1960). Ego Distortion in Terms of True and False Self. In The Maturational Processes and the Facilitating Environment, (1965). New York: International Universities Press, 140-152.

Winnicott, D. W. (1971). "The Use of An Object and Relating Through Identifications" pp. 86-94. In Playing & Reality. London: Tavistock Publications.

Films:

The Vanishing, (1989). Directed by George Sluizer, and written by Tim Krabbe.

Damage, (1992). Directed and written by Louis Malle. Based on a book written by Josephine Hart (1991), Ivy Books, New York.

Father of the Bride (1991), directed by Charles Shyer.

Father of the Bride (1950), directed by Vincente Minnelli.

Burnt by the Sun (1994), directed by Nikita Mikhalkov.

CHAPTER TEN ☙

Afterthoughts: In Conclusion

In addition to my profession as a psychoanalyst, and my deep interest in people, my life passions have always been film, music and dance. Watching films and writing about them has deeply enriched my life.

While sitting in the darkened theatre, we travel to other worlds, both geographically, emotionally and interpersonally. Films deepen our understanding of feelings, trials and tribulations, as well as joys and sorrows—everything that encompasses the human condition.

The "soul" purpose of writing this book is to discover and share the gifts that movies give. This includes helping us to understand the human mind and heart in its multitude of feelings and thoughts—crying, laughing, celebrating, mourning, losing, finding.

Cinema and music create a unique marriage. What we experience in movies is enhanced by the accompanying music. Music in films is powerful; soundtrack, musical score, and musical motif, communicate, emphasize, and deepen our understanding of, and connection to, the characters and actions in the film. Besides, music is visceral—it makes us move.

My mother said I danced before I walked. Music, a universal treasure, is an essential ingredient in life, dance and film. Shakespeare said, "If music be the food of love, play on…" As usual, Shakespeare got it right. Dancing has always been a special part of my life. Even during the current pandemic, my dance partner, Boris, and I roll up the rug and dance tango, mambo, cha-cha, waltz and foxtrot, in my living room, or in Central Park, New York City on a wooden stage in the summertime.

I think dancing and writing are similar in that they express rhythm, movement, feelings, emotions—or may carry you to some new place. When we allow ourselves to enter the world on the screen, we deepen our understanding of the movie, the characters, their feelings and conflicts.

So my invitation to all of you is dance. In whatever form it takes. Do it your way. Dance is a metaphor. Enjoy yourself. It's later than you think. As in Frank Sinatra's unforgettable words, "I did it my way."

Anita Weinreb Katz

GLOSSARY ❧

Explanation of Psychological Terms

Analysand – The person who is receiving psychological help from the psychoanalyst, is referred to as either the "the Patient" or the analysand.

Annihilation Anxiety – fear of no longer existing, or of being obliterated.

Compensate – substituting a behavior that is appropriate for an inappropriate desire.

Counter Transference – the feelings and thoughts that the therapist transfers or projects onto the patient.

Decompensation – a breakdown of defenses and normal adjustment; in psychology, the term refers to an individual's loss of healthy defense mechanisms in response to stress, resulting in personality disturbance or psychological imbalance.

Defense – behaviors that protect against painful or inappropriate behaviors or feelings; defense mechanisms are psychological strategies that are unconsciously used to protect a person from anxiety arising from unacceptable thoughts, feelings or behaviors.

Depersonalization – a state in which one's thoughts and feelings seem unreal or not to belong to oneself, or in which one loses all sense of identity. In a sense, a person becomes an "it."

Derealization – a mental state where you feel detached from your surroundings, in which people and objects around you may seem unreal.

Developmental Stages – Pre-oedipal (under 2 years old), mother-child connection and father-child connection; Oedipal (age 3 or 4, until 5) relationships are triangular - competition with one parent and bonding with the other, either father or mother, love for mother and hate of father, or love of father and hate of mother.

Disorganization – a state in which a person is or becomes disorganized, psychopathological inconsistency in personality, mental functions, or overt behavior.

Effectance – the state of having an effect on another person.

Enactment – behaving or acting in an inappropriate manner that relates to inner conflicts and desires and not to the realistic situation.

Existential – concerned with existence, and a condition that exists in the present, an ongoing present condition.

Fetishism – the attribution of inherent value, or magical powers to an object.

Identity diffusion – identity diffusion is one step in the process of finding a sense of self. It refers to a period when an individual does not have an established identity nor is actively searching for one. It is the process when a person is figuring out who they are. In adolescence when a person has not yet fully realized their social identity or defined their personality traits, and they are not actively seeking to.

Interpsychic – feelings or thoughts that occur within the minds of two or more people; an extended psychic dimension regarding the joint functioning and reciprocal influences of two or more minds, or individuals.

Intrapsychic – pertaining to impulses, ideas, conflicts or other psychological phenomena that arises or occurs within the mind, or the psyche of the individual.

Naturalistic observation – a research method that is used by psychologists and other social scientists to collect information (whether verbal or nonverbal) by observing people in their environment.

Oedipal Complex – (based on Freud's theory, derived from the Greek myth Oedipus Rex) the Oedipus complex refers to the young boy, falling in love with his mother, and having a desire, fantasy, or wish, to eliminate/kill his rival, the father. (The female equivalent of the Oedipal complex is the Electra complex, in which the girl falls in love with the father and wants to eliminate the mother.) Depending upon the sexual orientation of the child, this could refer to the same sex parent.

Oedipal phase – oedipal phase of development (from approximately age 3 to 5) involves the triangulation of love and competition in which the child loves and desires the parent of the opposite sex and wants to eliminate the other parent. The second oedipal phase usually occurs during early adolescence (around 11 or 12) with the same dynamic as previously mentioned, and in the best scenario it is resolved by age 13 or 14.

Perversion – the alteration of something from its original course, meaning or state to a different one.

Pre-oedipal phase – the pre-oedipal phase of development is from birth to age 2 or 3 and is a dyadic relationship between the child and each parent.

Primary-process – a process of thinking that is not governed by laws of logic, i.e. dreams. Dreamwork includes primary process thinking. The generally unorganized mental activity characteristic of the unconscious and occurring in dreams, fantasies, and related processes.

Reductionism – a theory in psychology centered on simplifying or reducing complex phenomena into their most underlying basic parts.

Screen Memory – a distorted memory generally of a visual rather than verbal nature, deriving from childhood. The term was coined by Sigmund Freud and the concept was the subject of his 1899 paper "Screen Memories."

Separation/Individuation – this term defines a stage of development when the child is capable of emotionally separating from his or her mother. It includes rebellion against mother/father, as well as a connection to the child's own feelings and ideas about him or herself, and those he or she is attached to (mother, father, siblings, etc.).

Transference – the feelings, thoughts and fantasies that the patient experiences in relation to the therapist; the redirection to a substitute, usually a therapist, of emotions that were originally felt in childhood. These are the feelings that the patient initially experienced in his/her/their childhood in relation to parents or other significant people.

Transitional Object – a physical object, such as a blanket, or teddy bear, that gives the child comfort and may temporarily substitute for the mother, or mothering figure.

"Dr. Dog" Christopher Robin

Christopher Robin, nicknamed "Dr. Dog" by one of Dr. Anita Katz' patients, was often present during sessions.

ABOUT THE AUTHOR ❧

Anita Weinreb Katz, PhD

Dr. Anita Katz is in private practice in psychoanalysis and psychotherapy in New York City. Anita Katz, PhD is on the faculty of the New York University Postdoctoral Program in Psychoanalysis and Psychotherapy, and at the Object Relations Institute. She is a senior member of IPTAR (Institute for Psychoanalytic Training and Research) and IPA (International Psychoanalytic Association). She is a clinical supervisor in the clinical psychology doctoral program at City University of New York. She has enjoyed and been enriched by the opportunity to present her work and to supervise psychotherapists in various cities in South America, Europe, Asia, Iceland, South Africa and the United States.

Dr. Katz has presented and published on aspects of psychoanalysis (both theory and practice) at institutes in China, London, Berlin, Dublin, Mexico City, New York City, San Francisco, Miami, Chicago, and California, between 1998 and the present.

She has presented at the American Psychoanalytic Association, on May 16, 1999, in Washington, D.C.; The Association of Psychoanalytic Psychotherapy, on September 9, 1999, in Mexico City, Mexico; New York University Postdoctoral Program in Psychotherapy and Psychoanalysis, on September 16, 2000; The Psychoanalytic Society of Long Island, on November 12, 2000; and the Object Relations Institute, on April 20, 2002, in New York City.

Among Dr. Katz's many national and international presentations, Dr. Katz presented in London on the film *American Beauty* directed by Sam Mendes on July 6th, 2003, at "The Life Cycle" conference of the British Psychoanalytical Society on the topic of *Family Knots and Abusive Ties*. At Trinity College, on July 27, 2002, in Dublin, Ireland, Dr. Katz presented her paper *"Transformations and Endings in the film American Beauty."*

On November 18th, 2000, IPTAR (Institute for Psychoanalytic Training and Research) celebrated its 40th Anniversary in New York City with a Conference entitled *"Contemporary Perspectives on Enactment, Gender and the Dynamic Unconscious."* On one of the panels that day, (which happened to be Dr. Katz's birthday), she presented her paper, *"Growing Up, Getting Stuck, or Breaking Down in the film American Beauty: Oedipal and Pre-oedipal Revisitations in Two Generations."*

In March of 2002, Dr. Katz presented a workshop sponsored by the Object Relations Institute for Psychotherapy and Psychoanalysis, entitled *Exploring Psychoanalytic Theory and Technique Through Cinema.* In April 2002, she presented at the Institute under the topic of "Passionate Attachments: Fathers and Daughters" entitled *"Fathers Facing Their Daughter's Emerging Sexuality."*

In March of 2005, Dr. Katz presented under the auspices of The Metropolitan Institute for Training in Psychoanalytic Psychotherapy. Her presentation, entitled "Rupture and Repair" delved into the process by which the rupture within the working alliance between therapist and patient was healed.

In 2018, Anita Katz co-edited a book with Arlene Kramer Richards entitled *Psychoanalysis in Fashion,* published by IPBooks. In addition, she wrote several chapters, entitled *Intimations of Youth and Unlimited Possibilities, Fashion Journey in Psychoanalysis: Looking As Well As Listening,* and contributed to the Introduction. People in the fashion industry as well as the field of psychoanalysis contributed other chapters.

Dr. Anita Katz has published many film and book reviews in several journals, including Psychiatry, Psychoanalytic Psychology, Psychoanalytic Review, Round Robin, and Psychoanalysis and the Arts, since the early 1970's.

Dr. Katz wants to thank Alma Bond, Phyllis Dischel, Ada Frumerman, Eve Golden, Roz Goldner, Lynda Gunsberg, Norman Handelman, Jennifer Katz, Stanley Lieberman, Ilana Litvin, Joan Oliner, Doris Pfeffer, Arlene Kramer Richards, and the Martin Bergmann Study Group for their thoughtful readings of early versions of many of her writings.

Anita's Family Photos

Anita with Dad

Anita with Mom & brother Marvin

Anita & Brothers Airplane

Anita—the center of her family

Anita at South Street Seaport, NYC - US

Anita and Brother Marvin

Anita the Dancer

Anita & Chimp in Russia

Anita's Family Photos

Brothers Joseph & Marvin

Ira Katz

A family conversation

Jennifer in Costa Rica

Mike & Jenifer's

Artie Cat & Jen

Jenny & Anita

Jenny & Kitten Fetchka

Anita & Jenny

Shanta Genia &

**Jennifer's elephant drawing for Anita (L),
with secret message behind the frame (R).**

Anita's Family

Anita & Brother Marvin

Jennifer & Anita

Jennifer

Anita with Family

Anita & Trainer Joel

Anita's red hot wheels

Jennifer with Dora

Jenny lecturing

Anita in Russia

CPSIA information can be obtained
at www.ICGtesting.com
Printed in the USA
BVHW020309170422
634472BV00001B/1